To Be A Good Printer

OVERLEAF

Richard Robert Donnelley
1836–1899

TO BE
A GOOD PRINTER

Our Four Commitments

by Gaylord Donnelley

The Lakeside Press
R. R. DONNELLEY & SONS COMPANY

To my brother,

ELLIOTT DONNELLEY

who gave so much to so many

Preface

You will not find a history of R. R. Donnelley & Sons Company in these pages, of which Company I am immensely proud, nor the story of my business career. I have no illusions as to my talents as an author, but my associates have taken advantage of my love for and my dedication to the Company and the thousands of fine people in it. They have persuaded me, in the year of my retirement, that it would be useful to present and future generations of Donnelley people to draw upon my experiences, and my knowledge of the business even before my time, in an attempt to analyze the factors underlying our extraordinary strength and growth. In these pages you will find a brief, simple portrayal of our Company's character, an explanation of our basic philosophy and policies, and a description of some practices that have served us so well for over a hundred years. In setting down these thoughts I have followed the outline of a film prepared for our 1975 Annual Talks with employees.

Our policies and practices did not just happen. They came about in the beginning because my grandfather, Richard Robert Donnelley, and his active and strongly supportive wife, Naomi, both deeply religious, believed in them and naturally lived and conducted a business accordingly. They felt that they were put on this earth to serve their Lord in the very best way they could, with His help, and the Golden Rule was very much their guide.

The title of this book was inspired by my grandfather's nightly prayer as a young apprentice: "Please, Lord, make me a good printer." He applied himself diligently, and his prayers were answered, for he became known, even as a young man, as one of the best printers in Canada, and later in the United States. He felt his calling was a combination of science, art, and a profession. The high ideals and standards of this remarkable couple have inspired and guided us to this day. While R. R. Donnelley & Sons Company and its predecessor partnerships and companies were for over ninety years a family-owned business, I remember on several occasions my grandmother saying in her quiet and dignified, yet forceful, way that the family's role was to serve the business, and not vice versa.

My grandparents' sons, Reuben Hamilton Donnelley, my uncle, and Thomas Elliott Donnelley, my father, learned their lessons well, by precept, example, and experience. They were thoroughly dedicated to maintaining our Company's character: honesty, integrity, industry, competence, as well as our pride in and dedication to producing a useful product of high quality. This character had to be diligently cultivated, carefully nurtured, and vigorously protected from even the slightest erosion. These fundamentals could never be disregarded for expediency to solve an immediate problem; one tiny tear in the fabric of company character and the whole cloth could very well unravel.

My father often recounted occasions where he had been strongly urged to compromise to avoid dire results or even catastrophe. His determination to stand by his principles, to ascertain carefully what was right, and then try to persuade others of his position, almost invariably won the day. His character, courage of convictions, intelligence, enthusiasm, and warm, friendly personality were a combination hard to beat. As he urged us to stand by our principles, with characteristic humility he also urged us to be sure we were right, after considering every other point of view, before taking a firm position. Then, he said, it was surprising how often, after a thorough exposition of his views, people came to agree with him, and how seldom, if ever, the predicted catastrophe occurred.

It might be well to describe the role Reuben H. Donnelley played in the development of R. R. Donnelley & Sons Company. It was a most active one for over forty years. His many talents, including quick wit, imaginative humor, and ability as a raconteur, combined with his brother "Ted's" talents to form one of the most effective brother teams in industry. Even though Reuben H. Donnelley founded other enterprises, notably The Reuben H. Donnelley Corporation (now a subsidiary of Dun & Bradstreet Companies), he remained a Vice President of our Company and maintained an office in the Plymouth Court plant until his death in 1929. Thomas E. Donnelley served as Vice President of The Reuben H. Donnelley Corporation until that date. He then became Chairman of the Board, serving until 1952, when I succeeded him for a short period during a top management reorganization of that company.

To clear up an often-asked question, there has never been any connection in the strictly legal sense between the two Donnelley companies. However, with much stock ownership in common, some common directors and officers, corporate headquarters in the same building, and the sharing of employee facilities and activities, the practical relationship was very close. With the removal of The Reuben H. Donnelley Corporation headquarters to the Prudential Building in 1956, and the subsequent merger into Dun & Bradstreet, the nature of the relationship was naturally changed, but has remained most friendly.

R. R. Donnelley & Sons Company is strictly a printer, and in competition with others has always been a supplier of printing services to The Reuben H. Donnelley Corporation, and more recently to other divisions of Dun & Bradstreet Companies.

Much of what I say about Thomas E. Donnelley applies equally to Reuben H. Donnelley with whom he worked so closely and to many others who have carried on our traditions and contributed so much to our Company's success.

As a background to what follows in this book, it would be well to bear in mind the nature of our business. It is mostly manufacturing, but somewhat different from other manufacturing businesses, in that it is almost entirely service-oriented. We proceed only when an order, instructions, and copy are in hand. We do not produce for an inventory or stockpile of our own. Only a few of our customers, mostly book publishers, hold our products in their own inventory.

Perishability, therefore, is the key word. Last week's *Time* magazine is not of much interest to the reader. A few days' delay in delivery of Sears, Roebuck catalogs could mean millions of dollars of lost sales, never to be recovered. A late telephone directory results in greater cost of directory assistance, user dissatisfaction with poorer service, and other problems. Fast, reliable schedules are a must. With the exception of Bibles and a few other books, we are usually dealing with a unique, different job every time we go to press. Many articles in encyclopedias must be revised annually to keep them up-to-date. The New York telephone directory may appear much like the Chicago directory, but the number of pages and each name differs, and there are many subtle variations in style unobservable to the untrained eye. The Penney winter catalog has contents and specifications quite different from the summer book. No two issues of *The New Yorker* are the same in contents or size; each edition is quite new. Each prospectus and registration statement prepared for submission to the SEC and distribution throughout the financial community is unique in its contents and timing requirements, with frequent changes before and during production. The wide variety of products, constantly and often suddenly changing, increases the challenge and interest we all experience in our work.

We all feel also that we are producing something useful, a real source of pride and satisfaction. Our business is in intimate proximity to the wisdom, the knowledge, the beauty, and the culture associated with the Bibles, the books, the encyclopedias, and the learned papers it produces. We are very much a part of the knowledge industry. And at the same time, through our magazines, catalogs, directories, and financial printing, Donnelley is dynamically involved in news, merchandising, communication, and industry—in fact, in the breath and heartbeat of the national and world-wide human community.

It seems abundantly clear that the philosophy, policies, standards, and practices that have evolved during the history of our Company have now as much value as ever, possibly more. While we have held to them firmly, we also have adapted them as needed to the ever-changing scene in our industry and society.

In looking at the basic characteristics of our Company for the purposes of this book, I am going to view them as commitments. A commitment is not necessarily written down, but is certainly felt in the heart and understood in the mind. It becomes very much a part of a person and his way of living and working.

The commitments dealt with in the chapters following are:

1. Our Commitment to Each Other
2. Our Commitment to Others Outside the Company
3. Our Commitment to Excellence
4. Our Commitment to Profit and Growth

Although these commitments are set out in separate chapters, they have no such clear lines of delineation. There is considerable overlap and interaction. The commitments are mutually self-supporting in countless ways, each gaining in meaning and importance because of its relationship to the others.

Obviously not everything of importance can be covered in a volume of this scope. However, if what is here will give some understanding of our heritage and principles and be of some guidance and inspiration for the present and future, I shall feel amply rewarded. And even more so if a better version can be produced by my successors.

Gaylord Donnelley

August, 1976

Contents

CHAPTER ONE

Our Commitment to Each Other

*The nature of our commitment to each other
frames and permeates virtually every aspect of
our operations. The way we work together,
how we identify and solve the many problems that
inevitably arise, how we select and develop our
people, the design of thousands of policies
and practices that guide our efforts . . . all these,
as well as much of what we find in our other
commitments, are functions of our commitment
to each other. In examining this commitment
to each other we shall examine first our basic
philosophy of working together; secondly,
the ways in which we find and develop the people
who work within this philosophy; and thirdly,
how this commitment to each other works
out when we translate underlying philosophy
into everyday action.*

Naomi Ann Shenstone Donnelley   1845–1934

A Basic Philosophy of Working Together

There is no doubt that the quality of Donnelley people has been more important than any other single factor in the growth and success our Company has enjoyed over many years. Other factors, including our commitments to others, technical excellence, profits, and growth, have been extremely important. But in the last analysis it has been the ability of carefully selected, thoroughly trained and personally competent, dedicated people, doing work they are proud of, that has carried the Company to progressively higher plateaus over many decades.

My father, T. E. Donnelley, my uncle, Reuben H. Donnelley, and their father before them, R. R. Donnelley, had a feeling and a respect for the individuality of people that has been reflected in every Donnelley Company policy for all of our 112 years. They and their managers *knew* these people who worked for the Company, called them by name, were interested in their families, helped them overcome their difficulties, and shared a kind of family relationship with them. And most important, they appreciated the work each person was doing and were personally concerned to see that employees were adequately rewarded, promoted, and encouraged each and every step of the way.

In our society today, there is an ever greater need for our kind of company in which the goals of the company and each individual in it are commonly shared. As people work together over a period of time to produce useful products in the best possible way, it becomes increasingly clear that common individual and company goals become a strong basis for the success of both.

When this sharing of goals is understood, employees can quite honestly begin to feel as if they are working for themselves, as well as with and for their associates. They are doing what they want to do in an environment they like and with people having common interests. Industrial psychologists now confirm that this kind of alliance of individual and company goals leads to organizational success. Much of what they are saying today is really just sophisticated intellectual phraseology to express some highly important people concepts that my father, my uncle, and their parents before them, instinctively regarded as a way of life.

People in large companies where individuality is not recognized can come to think of themselves simply as workers, as wage earners, even as faceless, nameless bodies with numbers that come and go at appointed times and do what they are told and paid to do. It is no wonder that workers in such an atmosphere often feel the only way to deal with management is through union representatives.

Donnelley's hiring policies and training procedures for almost 70 years consistently have been aimed at finding the best people available for any job openings and then giving them the best possible training for those jobs. Later, as they become qualified, they receive further training and development for better and more rewarding opportunities and greater responsibilities.

In the development of human character, heredity is but one element. Family experience and education are others. Our part is to provide the work environment and to emphasize motivation and training that further mold character. When our carefully selected people are put in situations where they are encouraged not only to do their best work at all times but always to try to do what's best for the customer—even when it means redoing a job—they then develop pride in their work, in themselves, in their associates, and in their company. This self-reinforcing and inspiring atmosphere encourages people to reach levels far above what they might individually.

WHERE THE BALANCE SHEET FALLS SHORT

As each year closes and we begin to prepare our annual report to stockholders showing all the assets and liabilities of the Company, we share with many other writers of annual reports an inability to describe in any meaningful way the value of people. The purpose of the report is to tell the stockholders how the company is doing and to show its condition as reflected on an auditor's balance sheet. But a balance sheet can only disclose the cost of the land we own, our buildings and equipment, our work in process, the money we have in the bank, the value of our stockholders' equity, and so forth. Words and pictures can show our buildings, our equipment, our products, and our people, but cannot adequately depict the real worth of that last irreplaceable asset—the thousands of Donnelley men and women whose skills, attitudes, pride, and dedication combine to produce the never-ending stream of fine printed products that pour from our plants.

In these pages I shall review some of the many important characteristics of the people who work in our Company, with particular attention given to the concepts that lie behind our "people relationships" at Donnelley.

THE PEOPLE AND OUR BUSINESS

In our service-oriented business, production requires a combination of a broad range of skills and talents. Also, the character of the products we produce substantially determines the kind of people who work here, as well as the atmosphere in which they work.

For many people, the challenge of continually producing new products on exacting schedules adds a dimension to their job satisfaction that may be hard to define, yet is easy for most of us in our business to understand. Even though the job of the printer is often tough and demanding, there is a thrill for such people in applying their competence and skills to an ever-changing succession of products. They apply themselves with industry and commitment in the face of difficult challenges. There is a confidence fostered by past triumphs that this job, too, will come out on time, be a credit to themselves and our company, and a source of value, pride, and satisfaction to the customer. Underlying the approach we take to our jobs is a sense of importance, of personal identity, of responsibility, and of dedication.

The vast range of skills and talents required to produce our products becomes more astonishing with every passing year. It used to be that when we listed "Compositor, Cameraman, Engraver, Platemaker, Pressman, and Binderyman," we had pretty well covered the crafts involved in the average printing job. But not today. This list of highly skilled crafts, each with its own apprentice training program, has reached well over one hundred.

All of these craft jobs require intelligence, talent, intensive training, adaptability, and dedication—all more highly developed than ever before. The craftsman's expert performance is our assurance, and our customers', of Donnelley quality in the final product and our ability to meet the challenges of the future.

The talents required to produce fine printing are not confined, however, to the craft skills. The finest work can be ruined by careless handling, and much of what we produce is quite fragile. Original copy, film, paper, printed signatures, work in process, and final product all require the utmost care when being moved or stored. Each person who receives copy, delivers plates to the pressroom, trucks signatures to the bindery, feeds them to the bindery line, or handles packages on the loading dock is a very important link in our production process. Managerial, sales, administrative, and professional skills also play a significant part in contributing to the final product.

PEOPLE RELATIONSHIPS AT DONNELLEY

I think the best way to describe our policies in regard to people relationships is to say that we do everything we can to encourage every individual person in the company to deal with every other Donnelley person on a direct, face-to-face, personal basis. This is a very simple statement but, when we consider its full meaning, the implications are enormous.

As I mentioned earlier, the roots of this important policy go back to the Company's earliest years. They were evident in memos and letters of my father and his father. From my earliest childhood, I recall conversations in which my father and grandmother expressed their deep concern for people.

I am sure that in large part this attitude toward Donnelley people was a reflection of my grandparents' and parents' deep religious convictions and Christian way of life. They were grateful for everything God had given them—even in the early years when it wasn't very much!—and that feeling never diminished as long as they lived. But, from the very beginning, their feeling of personal responsibility for the people working for Donnelley made direct and intimate communication with those people easy, simple, and necessary.

At home, father would often talk about individuals in the Company and how well they were doing; he sometimes mentioned their personal problems. He knew these things from personal discussions, which he always found easy and which the people in the Company learned could be easy for them, too. Father was as approachable as he was truly interested and understanding. Some people might tend to label this kind of interest as "paternalistic." In my mind he very definitely wasn't, but the label is not really important. Father regarded employees as people and did whatever he could to encourage thrift and self-sufficiency, but he did not want to dominate anyone's life. I well remember his critical remarks to his college roommate, and perhaps dearest friend, who headed a company that supplied housing as part of the compensation of its employees. To father, this was an example of deplorable paternalistic intrusion into one's life.

No one individual in Donnelley today knows every person in the Company, as that would be impossible in a company our size. There isn't anyone in Donnelley today, however, who doesn't have available easy and direct communication with people around him and above him at each and every level of the organization, whenever he needs it, right through to the President and Chairman of the Board.

Through three generations of management, direct people relationships have been the source not only of profound mutual respect and understanding among Donnelley people but also of tremendous job satisfaction.

Simple as this concept is—for people to deal with people as if they were people—it might be worthwhile for us to spend some time to examine it a little more closely.

We start with a fundamental belief that individual people are different. Each man and woman has different talents, abilities, skills,

energies, motivations, and ambitions. People have different tempera-
ments and different sensibilities. And because everyone responds dif-
ferently to slights, praise, criticism, and even to friendship, there is
no way to categorize human personalities except in big, broad swipes
that have little significance in dealing with any single individual.

Each person is distinct and made from his own mold, not identical
to any other person living or dead. Each deserves to be treated on an
individual basis. So, in dealing with the problems that inevitably arise
in the daily conduct of business, individual discussions and considerations are by far the best way to arrive at solutions and to clear up
misunderstandings.

An employee may have a question about overtime allocation,
vacation scheduling, work assignments, promotions, wages, fringe
benefits, or any of hundreds of other matters that may arise for a
variety of reasons. The simplest and best thing for that person to do
is go directly to his immediate supervisor, explain his problem or ask
his questions, and get the matter clarified then and there.

In many cases, the problem is actually a simple misunderstanding
that can be cleared up in a few words. If it is more complicated, the
supervisor may have to get additional information from other sources.
At times the problem may arise from a supervisor or someone else
in management having made a mistake. By raising questions, the
employee provides the opportunity for management to correct the
mistakes, thus benefiting not only the one who raised the questions
but others as well.

Sometimes, of course, there can be a continuing disagreement,
and perhaps for good reason. But, in our experience, in the vast majority of cases, problems are best resolved when employee and supervisor simply sit down and have a frank and open discussion, carefully exploring the reasons behind the situation or decision. At the
least, a better understanding on both sides usually results.

I have placed a great deal of emphasis on the need for *individual*
discussion, because this is critical to the entire thesis. When one employee attempts to speak for others than himself, or when several
employees claim to represent all employees in a confrontation with
management, the possibility of achieving mutual understanding and

reaching an agreement satisfactory to everyone is much diminished. I feel strongly that the individual employee who has the grievance is the best person to present it, and while he should always have the right to have another employee with him if he chooses, the most satisfactory solutions are those that represent a clear meeting of the minds between the employee and his supervisor.

There are other benefits to this approach besides its usefulness in solving problems. Individual discussions help the employee acquire greater self-confidence, a better understanding of the business, and of what is happening, and why. In many cases, he makes a real contribution to the solution of a problem; in others, he helps clear up misunderstandings. The solid working relationship with his supervisor that usually results from these discussions also does much to increase an employee's job motivation and satisfaction and to enhance the pride he feels in his performance.

PROVIDING THE CLIMATE

We can talk all we want about people relationships and about free and open discussion between the employee and his supervisor, but if the supervisor won't listen, if he is not an understanding and basically considerate person, if he sees himself as an autocrat whose word is law, if he doesn't consciously want to help every employee find fulfillment and satisfaction in his job—then he cannot meet his responsibilities as a Donnelley supervisor or foreman.

The most important member of management in maintaining a good industrial relations climate, in my opinion, is that first-line manager who, to many employees, is the Company. If the employee respects his foreman and has faith in him, he almost surely feels the same way about the Company. The foreman has the greatest opportunity to err, but he also is in the best position to see that our concepts are lived up to in practice. He must always be willing to listen and ready to take the time to deal with an individual employee's problems no matter how severe other pressures may be.

The responsibility range of the foreman in our plants is very wide. He has technical and equipment responsibilities; he is responsible for safety, good housekeeping, maintenance, schedule, costs, quality, and, above all, for people. Because people relationships at Donnelley are so important, our foremen play a most important role; they have a broad range of responsibility and authority.

In union shops, the foreman may brush off an employee's complaint by telling him to file a grievance or see his chapel chairman, but at Donnelley it is a primary responsibility of the foreman to *resolve* the problem, never to brush it aside. In committing a large part of his time to people, the foreman must deal fairly and have the ability to anticipate problems before they develop. He formulates and implements plans in terms of their impact on people, and is the key link between higher management decision making and the people on the floor. Of course, he also exercises correspondingly more authority. But when I speak of authority I do not use the word in any traditional sense of suggesting autocratic rule or a kind of irreversible power. I am talking about an authority based on an open-minded consideration of the facts, an authority based on knowledge and a willingness to consult with and involve others in the decision-making process, and an authority that understands the need to permit decisions to be reviewed by higher management in the event that the employee is not satisfied.

At times a foreman may feel overwhelmed by his responsibility burdens. At such moments if an employee walks in with a gripe, he may not get the friendly reception he has been led to expect and indeed is entitled to. But that should be a momentary lapse, a forgivable human failing on the foreman's part, to be made up for later. That's why he's a foreman at Donnelley—because he recognizes the importance of every individual in the Company and knows how to deal personally with every employee for whom he is responsible.

Another important aspect of a foreman's responsibility is his basic attitude. When the foreman sits down with an employee, he is there not as a "boss" (a term I have never liked), but as a sympathetic listener, as someone in a good position to be of help to another with a problem. That should be his attitude, which, in turn, should be evident to the employee. As the employee tells his story, or asks his question, the foreman should try not to interrupt, lecture, or contradict, but instead should listen and try to understand. In everything the foreman says and does he should recognize and respect the employee's importance as a person, as he explains his and the Company's position in clear, understandable terms. The supervisor should remember that no matter how trivial or mistaken some matter may seem at the time, the issue is important to the individual employee who brought it up.

Dealing with employee problems is just part of the supervisor's role. Where employees make unusually fine contributions, he must recognize individual achievement with words of encouragement, specific personal commendation, and, by no means the least important, the merit raise.

I don't mean to suggest that the foreman is alone in forwarding meaningful people relationships at Donnelley. Not at all. Everyone in management and staff has a real responsibility toward everyone in the Company with whom he comes in contact. It's just that the foreman or first-line supervisor is in the most critical spot for making our policy work or not work.

Of course, it isn't possible for anyone to be perfect always, but there is no doubt in my mind that in Donnelley we have one of the finest and ablest groups of supervisors in industry.

SOME SPECIAL PROBLEMS ASSOCIATED WITH GROWTH

When our Company was small, the first-line supervisor was the head of the company—R. R. Donnelley. Company policies weren't written down anywhere; they were simply in the founder's mind and heart. They weren't written down until the Company grew so big that, by my father's time, foremanship had to be shared with a number of other men. Today, with our multiple plants and divisions, there are literally hundreds of people in sensitive management positions affecting thousands of Donnelley employees. To their credit and the Company's, I am proud to say that their way of dealing with those thousands of important individuals is no less conscientious and concerned than was my grandfather's and father's in their times.

One of the greatest satisfactions of my long career with the Company is to realize that our present decentralization of twelve manufacturing divisions in ten geographical locations, organized in four groups, plus a corporate headquarters, enables us to maintain and cultivate today almost the same kind of individual recognition among plant personnel, management, and staff at all levels that my grandfather and father and their people had for two generations before us.

As we have grown and the number of our supervisors has multiplied, management lines of communications have been greatly lengthened. The possibility of misinterpretation of policy is negligible when supervisors are few, but it is a serious concern when they are many. To meet these problems we have continued to decentralize our management. We have established strong corporate staff services not only to assist divisions but also to use as an arm of general management to help insure continuing implementation of our employee relations policies.

We also have developed a broad range of training and communication programs. Our annual talks for employees provide top management with a particularly fine occasion for personal visits in our various plants and divisions, for meeting with employees and reporting to them the state of the business. We meet with our apprentice graduates to celebrate their achievement, congratulate them, and talk with them about our company and the future it holds for them. Our Service Recognition Programs include for twenty-five year veterans—and at every five years thereafter—an individual "coffee," a group dinner with management of all levels, a day off with pay, and an extra check for a celebration with the family. We have supervisory training programs that deal very thoroughly with basic human relations, and we have further training in grievance handling, merit reviews, and every aspect of our employee relations policies. At least once a year top management sits down with all managers in each unit for a give and take, question and answer session that usually lasts hours. All of these programs are carefully designed to meet the challenge of maintaining individual personal relationships in our growing company.

Another important factor in developing a good employee relations climate is communications. Employees must all know and understand company policies and procedures. Policies can't be kept in a book on the foreman's desk or in his head; they have to be posted on the wall, prominently, where they can't be missed. All of our employee relations policies and practices, including the rights of employees and the duties of supervisors, are clearly spelled out in a series of wall charts and employee relations manuals distributed through all our plants. For example, grievance procedures, which are clearly defined for all employees, include both formal and informal procedures. There are specific formal procedures for stating and presenting grievances, for providing answers, and processing appeals through to general management. Informal procedures follow the same route of presentation and appeal but do not require formal writeups and responses. A third important method of settling questions and complaints is found in our Open Door Policy, which plays a basic part in maintaining the climate we want.

OPEN DOOR POLICY

The Open Door Policy provides that if an employee does not want to talk to his foreman—if he doesn't want to follow the normal grievance procedure—he can go and talk to *any* member of staff, line, or general management who he thinks might be helpful.

One obvious problem in this policy is that it permits employees to go around or "over the head" of their immediate supervisors. This can cause resentment, particularly when the supervisor feels that he could have solved the problem just as well, or better and more quickly than the Chairman of the Board! But I have always looked on the Open Door Policy as a kind of relief valve. If the foreman has made a mistake or if the employee doesn't feel comfortable with him, or is reluctant to talk with him for any reason, it is extremely important that he have some other place to take his question or complaint—and that place must be one where the foreman's conduct or judgment will be scrutinized just as closely as the employee's. With years of experience, most foremen not only accept this, but feel reasonably comfortable with it.

Most people seem satisfied just knowing the opportunity is there. Of the people who have come to my office over the years, most came under our Open Door Policy because they felt they had a special problem that perhaps I could understand and help solve better than someone else. My first objective was to listen and learn all the thinking, feelings, attitudes of the person and the facts as he saw them. Then I tried to get the picture and facts from all other possible sources. Sometimes I was able to clear up a misunderstanding based on some misconceptions. Sometimes a mistake had been made unintentionally and could be rectified. In other cases, a new solution to the problem could be found. In still others, nothing could be done except to explain to the person why the situation was what it was and must continue so in the best interests of the business and all concerned. My experience with the Open Door has been duplicated hundreds of times by many other managers.

Another benefit of the Open Door Policy is that the nature and extent of open door appeals to higher levels of management can be an index to how well employee relations are being handled within the operating unit. I tend to be suspicious not only when there are quite a few, but also when there are very few.

The final thing required for a healthy employee relations climate is the right kind of employee. It doesn't do much good to have well trained supervisors and well defined policies and procedures unless the individual employee takes pride in his work, strives for self-improvement, has strong motivations, and respects others as well as himself; in short, is a fine person. How we find and help to develop such people is the subject of the next section.

* * *

Several years ago during a union drive at Crawfordsville, one of our employees was reported to have said that one reason she didn't want a union at Donnelley was that if she ever got mad at her foreman, she didn't want some union guy giving him hell; she wanted to do it herself.

When we think about this little incident, it tells us a lot. That woman felt free to say what she felt. She had the independent spirit to want to speak for herself, not have someone else do it for her. And I think she also knew that her foreman was the kind of person she could talk to, directly and individually. I think her remark expresses colorfully and well what this chapter is all about.

Finding and Developing People

Although our employee relations concepts have remained essentially unchanged throughout our history, our approaches to finding and developing people have undergone tremendous evolution and improvement in the face of changing needs and times. Sometimes it doesn't seem possible that in one person's lifetime—I'm thinking of my own sixty-six years—the entire world, and particularly our American society, could have changed as much as it has.

During my father's time the printing industry was undergoing changes, too, and the name R. R. Donnelley & Sons Company, The Lakeside Press, was becoming very well known, not only for the quality of its work and services but also for the experimentation and innovation in which the Company was constantly involved. My father had taken over as president of the Company upon the death of his father in 1899, and T. E.'s determination to make Donnelley the finest printing company in the country was evident in everything he said or did.

It was apparent particularly in his continual search for good people to work in our plant, to learn the printing business, and to help Donnelley grow. But those early years presented problems quite different from the ones we face today. In all of the trades—carpentry, bricklaying, plumbing—it was standard practice for young boys thirteen or fourteen years of age, just out of grade school, to take jobs assisting experienced craftsmen and, in that way, learn the trade themselves. This was true in the printing business, too, and Donnelley always had a considerable number of young boys in the plant on an apprentice basis. But my father wasn't satisfied that this was the best way to develop the finest printing craftsmen in the world, which was what he intended to have.

17

Just after the turn of the century, two major events led to the formation of our Donnelley Apprentice School. The first was the occurrence of four major strikes by printing unions, from 1903 to 1907, leading to our emergence as an Open Shop with no union-represented employees. No longer able to call on unions or union hiring halls for trained help, we set out to train our own craftsmen.

The second key event leading to the formation of our own Apprentice School occurred when my father went to England in 1907 to negotiate our first contract to produce the *Encyclopaedia Britannica*. While there, he learned of a special school for printing apprentices in France, near Paris, and arranged to visit it. Impressed with what he saw there, he founded the Donnelley Apprentice School in Chicago in 1908.

In a formalized school approach, father saw the many advantages of teaching craft skills in an organized and structured way, rather than simply associating young apprentices with experienced craftsmen in the hope that the apprentices would somehow pick up skills. Old-time craftsmen were not always eager instructors—often the opposite, withholding as much craft knowledge as long as possible. John Clyde Oswald, Publisher, *American Printer*, in addressing our 1916 apprentice graduation, might have been referring to similar earlier conditions in our plant when he said that, as an apprentice in Ohio, "Whatever information I got then, I had to steal!" I do know there has long been a strong tradition of our craftsmen sharing knowledge and actively teaching apprentices, though they were not above an occasional prank, such as sending the young man off in search of type lice.

The long-range benefits of the school, both for the students and for Donnelley, proved to be invaluable. The first school director had been a public school principal, and he worked toward what T. E. wanted in a curriculum. In both the pre-apprentice and apprentice programs, he was able to provide the boys with high school courses, such as mathematics, English, social studies, elementary mechanics, and bookkeeping, during half of their school day and printing craft instruction the other half.

Donnelley was already known in Chicago as a "good place to

work," and the school further enhanced our reputation. There were always more applications for admission than could be accepted.

As the years went by and public high school education became more available to more young people, Donnelley's standards for new apprentice employees also changed. By the time I first came to work in the late 1920s, most of our apprentices were selected from among high school rather than elementary school graduates. Today, with an increasing number of high school students going on to college, with others going into military service, and still others preferring a period of mobility before selecting a permanent career, many of our applicants for craft training are already in their twenties.

The apprentice program for many years has been the training ground for future Donnelley craftsmen, many foremen, and other managers. A number of our senior executives over the years have been its graduates, as have our salesmen, our estimators, and customer service representatives.

EVOLUTION OF SELECTION METHODS

Our primary objective in choosing people has always been, of course, to select the best qualified applicants for the jobs we had to fill and future ones we might develop. This is still true, in the sense that the basic character, apparent aptitudes, and general attitude of a person are key considerations. But just as our Company, in a fast changing society, has itself changed in size, technology, and organization, so have our methods of determining who among employment prospects is "best qualified."

So many of our past and present employees have made important contributions to our Company's success that naming the most outstanding ones would serve no useful purpose. I want to make an exception in the case of Mabel Rugg, however, simply because it wouldn't be possible to discuss the evolution of our selection methods without mentioning her. Mabel Rugg was one of the early pioneers in industrial testing and, through her, our Company also became a pioneer in this field. She had a rare talent of sensitive intuition and highly developed psychological skills, with a sound understanding of the limitations of testing alone.

At Mabel's suggestion our management permitted her, as an out-side consultant, to conduct an experiment with a small group of long-term Donnelley employees, each of whom was well known to our top management. Spending a limited amount of time with each of these employees, and using a combination of tests and interview techniques she had developed, Mabel evaluated each employee's capabilities and aptitudes. She then offered her analyses to management for them to compare with their own personal evaluations which had been formed through many years of working with these people.

Mabel's evaluations, based solely on her test-interviews, were so astoundingly similar to management's judgments that it was obvious she had much to offer our Company. Consequently, Mabel joined our Company first as a consultant and later, in 1934, as a fulltime employee. Her responsibility was to set up a comprehensive testing and evaluation program to help us identify more dependably those people already in Donnelley who had capabilities beyond their present jobs. This provided a new, better tool to help us predict success without a long period of on-the-job observation. It also reduced the risk of placement failure, and thus was in everyone's best interest. We have never believed in promoting someone whose qualifications for the new job were minimal in order "to give him a chance." This too frequently leads to disappointment, does the individual employee no favor, and is hard on the Company as well.

I believe this was the first such comprehensive evaluation program used in the printing industry, if not one of the first business applications anywhere. The method generally didn't come into vogue until the late 1940s.

Our primary use of Mabel's techniques in the beginning was in helping us to place our people in positions best suited to their talents and capabilities and to avoid misplacing them. As time went by, we extended application of the techniques to help us in our initial hiring decisions as well.

It should be understood, of course, that test results alone never determined what action the Company would take in hiring, placing, or promoting an individual. If an employee wanted to try out for a different job, he would first be tested and interviewed by Mabel. His prospective manager would then receive her report, study it along with his work record, and also interview the candidate. If the report did not support the placement, the manager might still assign the individual to the new job—that was up to the manager, as it still is today. The purpose of the personnel test and interview was to collect as much information as possible in order to help managers make better decisions, using all the other knowledge available to them.

A common fault of industrial testing in recent years has been the tendency of companies to rely too heavily on scores and academic records, and in effect to let numbers become the sole determinants of placement. The very finest tests are still only tools; they should never be regarded as substitutes for considered judgments and proven performance on the job. We give tests to help us determine an individual's fundamental aptitudes and abilities, in the hope that we can find work that will not only give the individual greater personal challenge and satisfaction but will also develop the individual and make him more valuable to Donnelley.

There are no tests that measure a person's energy, drive, ambition, willingness to make the extra effort, or persistence in holding to a goal regardless of the obstacles. Similarly, there are no tests for soundness of judgment, sensitivity to people, loyalty or integrity. Yet these are all important qualifications that we look for and want and hope to find in everyone we hire.

In recent years, our testing has been somewhat de-emphasized because it has become apparent that too great a reliance might be being placed on the scores. We have found cases where employees could sometimes perform well in a job despite test results to the contrary. Also, our tests often have proved more reliable for persons with good academic backgrounds, and thus experience with examinations, than for those with comparable potential but limited education. Lack of familiarity with testing somehow inhibits or distorts the person's response. This has made some tests less useful for our purposes.

In no sense have we abandoned scientific evaluation and aptitude testing but, having found some inadequacies in the tools we were using, we have been working to devise better ones. And we are looking for ways other than testing to give us the clues we need to help our people find the work they can do best and enjoy the most. In our efforts to select the right people for the right jobs, continued research and improvement in selection methods is fully as important as is developing new and better production processes and technology.

The teaching of craft skills first to elementary and later to high school graduates was the objective of our training program. The curriculum was different for grammar school than for high school graduates, being tailored to the trainee's academic and required craft skills in operating our plants. And since knowledge of plant operations was an important foundation for Donnelley salesmen, estimators and customer service representatives, as well as manufacturing personnel, the majority of our managers for many years were graduates of our Apprentice School. The growing need for staff specialists has reduced this percentage today, but the majority of manufacturing managers continue to be graduates of our apprentice training school.

Today, we still seek intelligent, industrious, and ambitious people to be printing craftsmen. And we still fill many of our management and sales openings with our own craftsmen. But the size of our business, growth of our technology, expansion of state and federal regulations, increasingly complex business methods, and development of Donnelley's decentralized line-staff organization all have combined to broaden our personnel needs far past those necessary at the turn of the century. While knowledge of plant operations is still very important, these changes, in the world and in the Company, have increased our need to search out people with specialist, professional and management skills.

Today, we look to college graduates for a variety of engineers, accountants, lawyers, business majors, and other specialists, as well as bright young people with liberal arts backgrounds. We need computer programmers and technicians and many craft skills that support, but are not directly a part of, the printing process. We require knowledge of chemistry to help us buy ink better and to develop new kinds of ink to serve our customers better, knowledge in metallurgy and chemistry for experimentation in platemaking, and knowledge of engineering for modifying presses, folders, and binders, designing buildings, and improving specifications.

To compete effectively in our increasingly complex society, we have lawyers whose specialities range across the many laws and government regulations affecting business life. A staff of writers, designers, and other artists provides our customers with assistance in creating the products we print. We have doctors and nurses to provide extensive medical service and we have people specially trained in the techniques of plant protection, industrial safety, pollution control, marketing, and relations services.

So, as we, America's major printing company, move into the last quarter of the 20th century, we need much broader talents than we did as the century began. We're not unique in this. Many growing companies in today's highly complicated business climate have experienced changing needs in personnel. But perhaps we are rather unique in the intensity of our continuing emphasis on craftsmanship. With all of our other needs, we still believe our most basic need is to find intelligent, capable people to become part of our team of exceptional printers who are dedicated to quality in our products, our service, and our human relationships, and who have the ability and desire to seek new technology and better methods, and to adapt their skills to resulting changes.

Hand tools have been replaced by much larger and more sophisticated machines, often controlled by computers, but the key element in attaining productivity and quality, the great common denominator that continues through the years, is the skill and dedication of the men and women who use those tools. How fortunate we have been to have thousands of dedicated people of various skills and professions who care and who are continuing to meet the challenge of accelerating change.

TRAINING AND DEVELOPMENT TODAY

The Donnelley training programs in the 1970s reflect dramatic changes in technology in recent years, as well as changes in the size and character and organization of our business. Training and development in the 1970s cannot involve simply the teaching of craft skills plus basic elementary academic subjects as it once did. Today we have training programs to fit all the many classifications of people we hire. Some come to us completely unskilled, others come with considerable technical, professional, or other specialized talent, but most know little about our kind of business. In every case, training at Donnelley, both on the job and in formal sessions, is designed to help take them from where they currently are in knowledge or skills to the farthest advanced point in the Donnelley organization that they have the willingness and ability to reach.

For employees who come to us from colleges, graduate schools, or positions in industry or the professions—such as lawyers, engineers, or computer specialists—our training is designed to orient them to our Company so they can understand our operations. Others bring with them knowledge and experience that will be of great value, particularly for jobs in manufacturing, once they have, by intensive training and study, achieved a thorough grounding in printing fundamentals. This is best accomplished by experience in the factory on the production floor learning the craft and working with craft people. The contacts they make, as well as the technical knowledge, will provide a firm base for their working life. Unfortunately, not too many young people today are willing to spend the time gaining this basic experience. We would like all Donnelley people to become "good printers."

At Donnelley we regard training as basically the responsibility of the manufacturing division or the corporate department to which the new employee is assigned. The training normally is given by persons who have other primary responsibilities. Our training staffs, consequently, play a supporting role and are relatively small at all levels. Overall training policy is determined and broad program guidance is provided by corporate management, but specific training programs are prepared and executed as a line responsibility within each division and department.

In hiring hourly employees we usually prefer people without previous printing experience so that we can train them in the Donnelley way from the very beginning. Virtually all the Donnelley people whom we classify as craftsmen today have come out of our apprentice training programs and were untrained in printing crafts at the time they were hired. Some of them have moved up through the semi-skilled ranks into apprenticeships; others, according to Company needs at the time, were hired directly as apprentices.

Once a Donnelley apprentice graduates to journeyman, his promotion to more complex and rewarding craft jobs is through our advanced craftsman programs. Most of this development is achieved on the job under the careful guidance and coaching of more experienced craftsmen and Donnelley supervisors. There is also periodic job rotation to assure maximum achievement and practice in all skills involved. In addition, journeymen may attend classroom sessions, enroll in correspondence courses, or do additional outside reading or project work.

Our apprentice program is still the most vital part of our entire training effort, and we are proud that it is the oldest such effort in our industry from the standpoint of its continual operation since its inception in 1908. It may also be the broadest such program in ours or any other industry, since today it embraces 106 specific crafts—many of them similar, of course, but each one having its own important differences and requiring its own special skills.

Today we have some 500 people in apprenticeships of various kinds. They have been carefully selected on the basis of character, intelligence, and special aptitudes and have been recruited either directly from the public schools, from our own unskilled or semi-skilled ranks, or from jobs elsewhere, as these young people believe our Company offers them greater opportunity. The training programs now span from two and one half to five years and their success can be measured by the fact that the great majority of our graduates spend their working lifetime at Donnelley. This has been true from the earliest days of the Apprentice School and it continues to be true, even in today's mobile society.

With the exception of craft training, the training given our sales people is certainly among the most comprehensive programs in our Company. New salesmen spend as much as six months, full time, in the training phase. During this time, they get product knowledge as well as training in sales skills.

As I have said, we believe that the first, or supervisory, level of management is the critical link between hourly employees and the higher levels of management. This is, therefore, the focal point at which management training programs are carried out. Because of this focus, first level management functions are similar to, and yet rather distinct from, functions of other managers.

At Donnelley, very few are hired directly from the outside as supervisors. This is partly because of the nature of our industry and particularly because of our own special methods of operating. We have found it better to develop our own employees for supervisory positions and, with this objective in mind, people are taught the basics of effective supervision before they are appointed. This assures an easy transition to the new job and, thereafter, maximum productivity as a supervisor.

In management training, the primary element is self-development in which the individual learns and grows on the job. To assist him in this, we offer various in-plant programs around which he (or she, of course), with the help of the supervisor, can plan personal further development. In special cases, we will sometimes sponsor an individual's participation in programs outside the Company that train and develop selected people having high potential for further advancement. These include advanced degree and university executive development courses.

Management development is thus accomplished by a composite of methods, including performance on the job, observing more experienced employees and managers in action, job rotation, participation in meetings and conferences, independent self-study, and formal classroom sessions—either in-plant or outside. Job rotation isn't always popular. No manager likes to break up a winning team, replacing a proven star to take on an untested newcomer who may take some time to attain full effectiveness in his new job. Not to do so, however, deprives the individual of developing his full potential for advancement, and the Company of a supply of broadly trained people well qualified for promotion to greater responsibilities.

On the other hand, it must be observed, Donnelley has never been or ever desired to be an inbred organization. In the Company's earliest days, all kinds of talent, including craftsmen, were brought in from the outside, usually permanently, but sometimes on a temporary basis for peak periods. It is a matter of policy that no qualified person within the organization is ever knowingly passed over to fill an important position in favor of an outsider. But with all the innovation, experimentation, and change that have continually been taking place, it is difficult to find within our own ranks all the kinds of knowledge and experience that our progress constantly requires.

We've come a long way since my early days with the Company, and our recruiting, selection, training, and development have indeed become increasingly sophisticated. But our goal is still, as always, to recruit the best possible candidates for our job openings, present or future, to train them for maximum effectiveness in their jobs, and to help them qualify themselves for future opportunities. In this we firmly believe that learning-by-doing in a succession of jobs, involving lateral transfers and promotions with ascending responsibility and complexity, is the essence of any human development program.

Commitments in Action

Once we establish the policy framework, once we select and develop certain kinds of people, what are the results? What happens? What is the outcome in terms of people and the company as a whole? How do our commitments to each other actually work out when we translate underlying philosophy into everyday action?

ATTRACTING AND HOLDING QUALIFIED PEOPLE

As I have previously indicated, I believe the nature of our business, the general working atmosphere we provide, and the careful selection and development processes that we have used over the years have permitted us to attract, develop and hold a tremendous number of high-quality employees.

In 1975 our average total employment was about 11,700. Some 6,700 of these Donnelley people have been with us for more than ten years, and over 2,200 have served for twenty-five years or longer, thus reflecting the impressive percentage of our people who choose to remain with us throughout their working lives. Two hundred and five Donnelley people served in World War I; four were killed in action. Of the 201 survivors, 196 returned to the Company when the war ended. Later on, during World War II, some 1,400 Donnelley men and women entered the military services and forty-three of them lost their lives. Of those who survived, more than eighty-five percent—some 1,150—returned to our Company when they were discharged. We must have been doing something right.

This stability of employment has enabled us to maintain an excellent blend of age, with the maturity and judgment it brings, and youth, with its vigor and enthusiasm. Our ability to attract and hold good people has other far-reaching results, an important one being our ability to move plant-oriented people into our management. More than half of our manufacturing management have been developed from among our hourly employees. About half of our division directors have risen from craft ranks to head manufacturing plants. Others who started as apprentices have reached top staff and sales positions; and one man who started as an apprentice many years ago recently retired as a Senior Vice President and a member of our Board of Directors.

ABILITY TO IMPROVE

Another area where our employee relations policies have played a major role is in our continuing effort to improve. Our ability to install new and improved equipment, our freedom to train and develop people in new processes and new methods, the willingness of our people to devote themselves to new tasks and new challenges ... all of these have played a major role in maintaining the competitive strength of the Company.

When some people think of improving technology, or automation as it's also called, they tend to think in terms of large layoffs or separations of employees. Fortunately, our record at Donnelley has been very good. On those occasions where we have seen that improved technology was going to cause a restructuring of jobs, we have formed special task forces to formulate a variety of special techniques and programs—all very carefully designed to cushion the impact on employees. These programs include comprehensive reassignment and retraining of people, special transfer programs, supplemental retirement benefits to encourage early retirement, and, on rare occasions, special separation pay programs. In the great majority of cases we have been able to avoid separations and have preserved employee job security.

Over the long pull, of course, our ability to lead technologically is very much a key factor in maintaining job security. Any attempt to maintain old methods where better ones are available would be short-sighted and self-defeating for our people, as well as for the Company as a whole.

SOME IMPORTANT INTANGIBLES

When thousands of people are working together in a complex organization, there must be some rules, regulations, and standardized procedures established, but with us these assume an important but low profile. High quality standards, exacting schedules, many highly specialized skills, individualized products, and the pride we can take in the usefulness of what we produce all tend to provide a high sense of self-discipline and to keep us on our toes day in and day out. Highly dedicated, cooperative people seem to understand well what is expected of them to get the job done with a minimum of supervision. This is discipline at its best and highest, even though it may not be what people usually think of when they hear the word with its unfortunate connotation of strict rules and severe penalties. In my early years throughout the offices and plants hung a number of signs: "The Business is Boss." That says a lot about our way of going then and now.

Much of what we do at Donnelley is keyed to the dedication and cooperation of our employees. We have seen time and time again the marvelous way in which our employees respond to challenge. In Chicago in 1967 when the city was literally closed down under tons of snow, many employees fought their way to work, stayed on the job for long hours, slept in the plant, and otherwise demonstrated a dedication to getting the job done that is, in my experience, unmatched in the industry. Unmatched, except perhaps by our employees in Mattoon, who demonstrated the same kind of dedication when that city was paralyzed by a blizzard six years later.

In Willard, Ohio, several years ago, the plant was struck by a tornado. Everyone pitched in, disregarding personal problems, and worked around the clock to clean up, mend, and get back in operation quickly so as to meet our customer commitments.

These are big dramatic examples, but over the years I have known of hundreds of others where extra care and extra dedication have supplied that extra something so essential to quality and schedule. There is little doubt in my mind that the close working relationships that are developed at Donnelley are keyed to the dedication and cooperative attitude of our employees. Our energy is not consumed in internal struggle. Employees and supervisors who learn to like and trust each other and learn to work together form an unbeatable team when the chips are down and the going is toughest.

EQUAL OPPORTUNITY

With regard to equal employment opportunity, I think it fair to say that Donnelley is in the forefront. We have moved with great conviction, not only to express our policy of fair and equal treatment without regard to age, race, color, religion, sex, or national origin, but to insure that this policy is being carried out at all levels in the Company. Our responsibility goes beyond the mere avoidance of discrimination; we are committed to taking effective affirmative action to provide equal opportunity for all.

Much of the progress we have made in this area results, in my opinion, from the general climate in our Company. Our people work together as individuals, respecting their fellow employees as human beings, as well as cooperating on a working team. It is difficult for prejudice to survive in this kind of environment.

THE EFFECT IN THE MARKETPLACE

By now, it must be very clear that the quality, dedication and cooperation of our people have a very substantial impact on the competitive strength of the Company. Often as I have taken customers through our plants and have shown them our facilities and our equipment and our people at work, I have received the highest compliments regarding the people who work here, their obvious skill, their attitude, their vitality, the dedication that is readily apparent to these visitors. All of these factors add to our competitive strength and our ability to convince customers that they are making a wise decision when they place their printing at Donnelley.

JOB SECURITY

Many things contribute to job security, but the single most important factor is customer demand. Unless buyers of printing decide to place their business with our Company, we cannot provide job security. Accordingly, virtually everything I have been discussing so far—the cooperative working atmosphere we work so hard to develop and maintain, the quality of the people we select, the concentrated training programs we provide, our never-ending efforts to improve—all these, as well as other commitments to be discussed later, contribute to the competitive strength that brings in the business that is the foundation for employee job security.

There are, of course, other things that management does to maximize job security. A brief review of our manning policies, workload fluctuations, and adjustments for work or equipment changes demonstrates our continuing preoccupation with employee job security.

1. *Manning Policy*—In virtually every department within our Company there are certain periods when workloads are considerably heavier than they are at other times, even though we try to attract customers who provide reasonably level activity throughout the year.

Many companies in our industry prefer to increase their manning each time they have a sharp rise in their production volume. When their production volume begins to fall off, however, these firms face a difficult decision. They must either lay people off, or go on a reduced work-week to spread their available work among the larger number of employees, or incur heavy no work costs, which may impair their financial strength.

We prefer to adhere to a manning schedule that will assure maximum employment security across the board. By hiring the number of people we feel are necessary to meet normal production requirements, we are generally able to handle both the production peaks and the production valleys. Peaks, generally, can be met by working overtime and by temporary transfers. This means higher overtime costs for the Company but helps us avoid later layoffs when the peak is past. When we hit a production valley, we are often able either to transfer people from one department to another to help meet spot emergency workloads—or possibly to schedule vacations. Our marketing and sales people, of course, are fully aware of these problems and do everything within reason to provide work that will fill in production valleys. Only as a last resort do we cutback to a shortened work-week.

This does not imply that we are perfect in setting manning levels; we are human and are subject to error. Occasionally, in spite of our best efforts, we may err in our forecasts, unexpected productivity problems may develop, our customer requirements may change, or national economic conditions may shift suddenly. The result may be excessive overtime or perhaps unusually low production periods.

Overall, however, we firmly believe our basic manning policies work very well over the long run and provide greater employment security for our people.

We firmly believe that the interests of our employees and our customers alike are best served through our manning philosophy and practices.

2. *Temporary Workload Fluctuations and Minimum Work-week—* Even with our carefully controlled manning policy, we periodically are faced with workload reductions due to seasonal, economic, or other causes. Our basic policy in these situations is to see it through together by extending a three-day minimum work-week guarantee to virtually all our employees (the only exception being some of our very short service employees). Significantly, this policy was developed in the early 1930s during a depression when our confidence in our ability to survive economic hard times was less than it is today.

We went pretty far afield in earlier days to keep from laying off employees. Just after World War I we found ourselves packaging chocolates, assembling boxes of Tinker-Toys, and hand-cleaning and re-labelling a boatload of cans of sardines that had been salvaged from a sunken ship. Perhaps the most spectacular example of these efforts was our ill-fated venture into the cigar-making business! Here, we decided, was a product that utilized many people in the manufacturing process. Furthermore, we could do our own selling. We imported two expert cigar-makers from Havana to teach our people how to hand-roll cigars. Ollie Sperry, a connoisseur of fine cigars and later a major executive, was in charge of that project. He maintained that our "La Patina" cigars were really of the finest quality. (He found only once a hairpin in a cigar!)

The only hitch was that we didn't know how to merchandise our product. After producing over 50,000 cigars, we discovered that cigar stores accepted them only on consignment and wouldn't pay us for the cigars until they had sold them to their retail customers. And, who had ever heard of La Patina cigars? In those places where our product finally did acquire some acceptance, the demand for more cigars always came just at the time when our people were busy getting out our mail-order catalogs! Suffice it to say that we never became a major factor in the cigar market.

The minimum guaranteed work-week, providing three days' work or pay each week, was established originally in 1933 in the depths of the depression. This guarantee has been renewed annually, and though it does not have nearly as much application today as it did then, it is much better than layoff and separation, since it keeps our people in an employment situation and preserves their benefits which would otherwise terminate on separation. While it does permit separations for long-term and permanent severe workload reductions, there have been only two times in a period of more than four decades when such separations were employed. These occurred in 1971 and 1972, in connection with the unfortunate discontinuance of *Look* and *Life* magazines. We did our best to soften the blow for a maximum number of individuals through offers of augmented early retirement, special supplemental separation pay programs, retraining, and transfer, sometimes unfortunately to a lower skill when that was the only opening. Later some were restored to their former jobs.

The nation's economy as a whole and our business in particular have been sufficiently strong since the depression of the '30s, so that we have very seldom found it necessary to drop down to the three-day guarantee. The existence of the policy today does, however, reflect our continuing concern

with doing everything we can to provide the finest job security for our employees.

3. *Equipment Changes and Work Transfers*—There are, of course,
other situations where the Company retains certain work, but
where the equipment used to produce the work is changed or
the work is transferred to another plant location. The following are two examples of the effect of technological changes
and our means of dealing with them, as discussed more generally earlier in this section. In the early '60s, we phased out
most of our letterpress operations in Crawfordsville as we
converted *World Book* production to offset. Also, in more recent years, to meet competition and hold the business, we
have been transferring telephone directory work from Chicago
and Crawfordsville to new plants designed especially for telephone work. In these equipment-change and work-transfer
situations, we have been uniformly successful in designing and
implementing a variety of transfer, retraining, and other programs so as to avoid forced separations.

I have spent a good deal of time on job security, partly because
it's such an important part of our total commitment to our employees.
While it's a complicated subject, overall I think we have good cause
to be proud of our record in this area.

WAGES, BENEFITS, AND WORKING CONDITIONS

Our basic policy with respect to wages, benefits, and working
conditions is simply to make each Donnelley location foremost as a
place to work. In all our plants, virtually all rates of pay compare
very favorably to those generally paid in the same area for the same
level of skills, and relate realistically to our competitors in other
areas. Our good pay rates, along with steady employment and a fair
amount of overtime, combine to produce good weekly paychecks
and high annual earnings. In one of our plants some years ago,
several employees moved to another town to get higher wages in an
automobile plant. They returned several months later asking to come
back. When asked why, they said that they liked the higher rate but
the hourly rate simply wasn't multiplied by enough hours.

Pay scales are reviewed at least annually at each plant. These reviews are based on exhaustive studies and analyses conducted by both plant and corporate staff personnel and are thoroughly reviewed by general management.

We have every reason to believe that our total benefit program, developed over many years, is the finest in our industry. It includes a Sick Benefit Plan, a Long Term Disability Income Plan, Comprehensive Medical Insurance (including Major Medical), Group Life Insurance, a Retired Employee Major Medical Plan to integrate with Medicare, and a Retirement Plan that we have every reason to believe is the very finest in our industry.

In characterizing our benefit package several points deserve mentioning. First of all, we work very hard to maintain and encourage employee interest in good plan design and administration. To this end, all plans were contributory for many years. Today, the Company is picking up most of the cost, but we use deductibles and co-insurance, not only because they discourage plan abuse, but also because they permit us to direct more money into higher coverages so sorely needed in major catastrophe cases.

When we say we have every reason to believe we have the finest benefit package in the industry, the assertion is certainly a rather broad one. With thirty-some thousand firms in the industry, we can never be absolutely sure ours is the best. But we do conduct frequent, highly detailed surveys to stay on top of the subject, and so characterizing ours as "the best" is more than a guess; it is based on considerable research.

Today, with several union pension plans in our industry going broke, the funding of our retirement plan deserves special attention. Too frequently over the years, in my opinion, many unions and employers have been too eager to brag about high benefits and have ignored or paid too little attention as to how to provide adequate funding over the long pull. Through the years we have taken great care to put money into the fund as benefits are built up so as to ensure that adequate money is there to pay retired employees when the time arrives for them to receive benefits. This practice is only now required by Federal law. Occasionally, over the years, a few people have criticized our funding as being too conservative, saying that we have been putting in more money than was needed. As I now see many printing union members being denied retirement benefits they thought they had earned, I take great pride in the fact that our employees can look to a very soundly funded plan as a source of their retirement income, in fact one of the soundest in all industry.

In addition to sound funding, I think we can take pride in the fact that the vesting provision established in our own retirement plan was generally more favorable to the individual than the requirements of the Pension Act of 1974. I, personally, still think that a thirty-year entry age with a higher yearly benefit, as originally provided in our plan, is better than entry at twenty-five, as now required by law. The younger person is less interested in retirement and is more mobile; the later entry into the plan permitted concentration of resources when they were most needed.

Over many years our fringe benefits have been carefully designed to help employees take care of themselves without our intruding into their personal affairs. We have tried to encourage thrift, not only through savings bonds programs, but also through a credit union and a savings and loan association in Chicago and savings deposit plans in other divisions. In the old days we actually deposited a dollar a week in savings accounts for apprentices so that graduating teenage apprentices had good savings accounts established, but this program was abandoned as apprentice wages moved up, as average age increased, and as many began to develop families during, or even before, the apprenticeship period.

As far as working conditions are concerned, customers who have visited plants all around the nation have often told us that our working conditions are outstanding in the printing industry. A constant effort is made to keep our plants and offices clean and orderly. It is hard to see how people could be expected to work safely and maintain productivity and quality otherwise.

Safety has been stressed for generations. It is not only a basic management responsibility, but each department has its own safety committee which looks for possible hazards in its daily work. Safety engineers take an even more professional approach, drawing upon their own training and experience. In establishing the policies of our business, we constantly are faced with questions of emphasis and priority. At Donnelley we have throughout my lifetime recognized safety as our number one priority, followed by quality, schedule and cost. Our commitment to safety is, I believe, confirmed by the safety records of our various plants. Most have run up safety records with no lost-time accidents through millions of man-hours without interruption. Our Crawfordsville Division holds the all-time record for the printing industry—9,611,563 hours. Industry statistics available to us indicate we are far out in front of our industry in this most important aspect of plant operations. In 1974, the most recent year for which statistics are available at this writing, the printing industry as a whole suffered 8.95 disabling injuries for each 1,000,000 man-hours worked. Our rate at Donnelley was 2.1. Therefore, when the Federal government rather recently entered the field with the establishment of OSHA, the impact on our Company was not significant.

Health concerns all of us, but neglect of it can severely handicap our operations, as well as cause individual suffering. All our plants have medical facilities with doctors and nurses in attendance (or readily available) for testing, first aid, emergencies, and consultation. This treatment is very well received, but we are careful not to get in the way of the individual's relationship with his personal physician.

EMPLOYEE ACTIVITIES AND RETIREMENT POLICIES

The Company encourages its employees to join together in a great variety of leisure-time activities. These include social events like dances and family picnics, organized sports such as basketball, bowling and softball, a great variety of hobby activities from chess through angling and photography to choral singing, and low-cost outings ranging from an evening at a baseball game to ten days in Spain. These activities are run by the Donnelley Clubs (Lakeside Press Employees Association in Chicago), which are assisted financially by the Company.

Our concern for our employees does not end with their retirement. We are quite aware of the problems inflation can create for retired people, even those who are members of very good retirement benefit plans, such as Donnelley's. From time to time we have therefore, voluntarily and at considerable expense, increased the benefit payments being received by all our retired employees. Retired employees who are not yet eligible for Medicare receive continuing coverage by a major medical insurance plan, with the Company bearing the entire cost. We also publish an annual Directory of Retired Employees, maintain a regular column devoted to retirees in the Company magazine, and encourage social activities among them.

POLICY TOWARD UNIONS

In attempting to gauge the full significance and impact of our employee relations policies, it seems appropriate to take a look at the whole question of our attitude toward unions—especially in our industry, where the gap between typical union and open shop operations is particularly wide and meaningful.

The impact of our open shop policy would not be nearly as large as it is were it not for the prevalence of highly restrictive work practices that printing unions have imposed on so much of our industry. Restrictions on hiring, training, crewing, overtime, transfer of people across jurisdictional lines, installation of improved equipment and processes . . . all these and many other restrictive work practices burden a great part of our industry. In many cases these restrictions were born more than a century ago but survive to undermine the job security and well-being of workers today. Any realistic evaluation of our growth over the years must take into account the competitive implications of restrictive work practices in our industry.

Over the years a number of people, particularly those who have been affiliated with union organizing drives, have characterized our Company as being "non-union." A more proper term is "open shop," in which employees are free to join or not to join a union.

A little background history helps explain our present position. Up until the Feeders Strike in 1903, R. R. Donnelley & Sons Company operated as a "union shop," but not as a "closed shop," where none but union members could be employed. In fact, non-members were employed, probably in a minority, and the Pressmen's contract expressly provided for this. My grandfather and father originally seemed quite comfortable with this situation. The strikes of 1903–07, with their accompanying violence and demands for a closed shop that would force union membership on all our production employees, led to the realization that the employment of any union members would undoubtedly result eventually in a closed union shop. The various restrictions imposed by union rules would have impeded the Company's development as a national printing company, and so my father concluded the Company could operate successfully only as a non-union shop. Since the 1930s, when the law was changed, our employees have been free to join or not join unions, as they saw fit.

We believe that employees at Donnelley should be free to elect union representation if they so choose. But we also believe that Donnelley people are going to be much better off in the long run if we are capable of running the kind of company in which employees do not feel it necessary to elect a union agent to conduct their dealings with management. Our deep convictions in this matter are keyed to four main considerations:

1. *Problems Inherent in the Agent Relationship*—Once a union is elected an agent of a group of employees in a particular unit, it becomes the legal bargaining representative of all those employees, whether or not an individual wishes such representation, and management comes under a legal obligation to deal through the union. In most matters relating to wages, hours and working conditions, management basically is not permitted to deal directly and individually with employees. Thus, the election of a union agent throws up a kind of iron curtain between the individual employee and his supervisor.

In placing themselves between management and employees, the unions simply are trying to justify their positions as agents. In so doing, the union leaders rather naturally tend to paint management of the company as an enemy of the employees. Thus, the union leaders have a kind of vested interest in doing everything they can to separate employees from their managers and somehow to suggest that the company and its management are exploiters of the employees. In a practical sense, I suppose I should not really criticize union leaders for doing this. Their actions in trying to drive employees and management apart are inherent in the system itself. After all, how can we expect a man who is being paid to be someone else's agent to encourage employees to handle their own problems?

I think one of the most unfortunate developments in American industrial life over the past forty years has been the separation of management and employees. What a paradox it is that in so many companies unions have actually been able to convince employees that their supervisors are their natural enemies and that employees can somehow advance their own interests better by joining in unions with employees working for our competitors.

At Donnelley we believe that all of us have a deep mutual interest in the competitive success of our Company and, accordingly, we believe that all of us have a tremendous interest in working together to meet our competitors and succeed in the never ending competitive race.

Further, unions tend to represent groups of employees by occupation, department, or other organizational unit. We simply do not want to deal with our employees as large homogeneous masses. We believe employees are different, that they have individual motivations, and that their problems and questions deserve to be dealt with on an individual basis. Accordingly, our deep convictions regarding the need to deal with employees directly and individually simply do not permit us to take a neutral position with respect to unions at Donnelley. We do not want to deal with our employees through unions and, accordingly, we make it very clear to our employees that while they are free to join, we sincerely hope that they do not feel it necessary to do so.

2. *Union Leader Ambitions and Objectives*—Once a union becomes the legal bargaining representative for employees, the whole picture becomes complicated by the personal motivations and objectives of the union leaders.

The union leader rather naturally is first interested in his own job and position. Finding ways to maximize income from dues and assessments, forcing membership through compulsory union shop contract clauses, building powerful political alliances—all these assume a high priority for the union leader even though they have little or no interest to the individual worker. All too frequently the welfare of the local union and the individual worker are sacrificed to the more personal ambitions of the union leaders.

In case after case we also find examples where union leaders think in terms of what is best for the big international union rather than a local, or what is best for certain kinds of workers, even though it may hurt others in the union. There have been some unfortunate cases in our industry in which printing union leaders have seemed to be more interested in protecting the welfare of employees in other companies than they have in furthering the best interests of employees whom they are obligated to represent in a particular company. Thus, union members in one company have been sacrificed for the good of union members in other companies.

3. *Restrictive Work Practices*—The third consideration that leads us to oppose union representation at Donnelley has to do with the far-reaching effects of the restrictive work practices that characterize so many of the union shops in our industry. These work practices have a substantial impact on the competitive cost structure and competitive strength of various companies. Our freedom from these restrictive work practices is one of the key factors in our Company's success.

Among the many freedoms we enjoy at Donnelley is the ability to select our own people in numbers and for qualities based on Company needs and to train them in our methods and traditions. We are free to establish fair manning without wasteful featherbedding and to install better equipment, methods, and processes. Further, we are not burdened with jurisdictional restrictions; we are free to transfer employees to other jobs when that will keep people working. And we are free to deal with our people in direct, individualized ways so essential to the development of a smooth-working, dedicated team. In all these and countless other ways, we and our employees are able to operate free of union shop restrictions. All of these freedoms contribute beyond measure to the competitive strength so essential to company business and individual job security.

4. *Destructive Strikes*—And finally, we are totally committed to the open shop because of the way in which all of us, including our employees and our customers, have been free of the vicious effects of strikes. I earlier have mentioned the perishable nature of our products and the virtually absolute need for them to reach the marketplace on schedule. Because the product is so perishable, the impact of strikes on customer, company, and employee in our industry is particularly serious. A customer would hesitate to commit all his printing requirements to our Company if he felt we were subject to work stoppages. Here again, as in the case of our freedom from restrictive work practices, our freedom from strikes is of tremendous competitive importance. Indeed, the competitive value of this freedom is multiplied both by the nature of our industry and the prevalence of strikes in printing union shops.

Some people, largely union leaders, like to suggest that open shop companies see the open shop as a way to maintain low wages and substandard working conditions. We believe just the opposite. The open shop has made possible the kinds of working relationships and operating methods that produce solid values for our customers and strengthen the competitive position of our Company. In this way the open shop has given us the opportunity to provide our employees with outstanding earnings, benefits, and working conditions.

I have cited the reasons and thinking behind our Open Shop Policy and our Company's attitude toward unions. The reader may well ask how all this has worked and how well employees understand their own stake in our Open Shop Policy. There have been several tests over the years.

During World War II, five unions were able to obtain elections in our Chicago plant. One lost the election; two of those who won shortly went on strike and permanently withdrew so many members that they no longer represented majorities. The response from the other two who won was also predictable. In an effort to impose a closed shop on us, the pressmen struck in June, 1945, and the lithographers respected their picket lines. Many did cross picket lines, and with the help of managers and office personnel, the plant continued to operate. By the end of two weeks, about eighty-five per cent of our employees were back at work and operations returned to normal. The two contracts reached subsequently—one from arbitration and the other from negotiation—generally reflected and were written around our prior operating practices.

Over the years, employees gradually lost interest in these two unions. We have not had a contract with one since 1948 and the other since 1963. For some years now we have neither negotiated with, nor recognized, either of these unions.

In more recent years, we have had one other very major test. From 1968 to 1971, a full-scale organizing campaign was mounted by all of the major graphic arts unions working in combination, with initial help and direction from Walter Reuther's Industrial Union Department of the AFL-CIO. The unions set up headquarters in each of our various plant towns, assigned thirty-five to forty organizers to this effort and, according to their own accounts, spent several million dollars trying to sell unionism to our employees. Donnelley employees reacted to all this union activity by not even requesting an election in any department in any plant.

Why did Donnelley employees turn back this major union thrust? I don't think anyone knows fully, but I believe there are at least two reasons that deserve to be mentioned here.

First of all, I think the unions made a very serious mistake when they revealed in published statements that the major reason for their drive on us had little to do with the welfare of Donnelley employees as such, but was, instead, designed to impose the union shop way of life on us so that we would lose much of our competitive strength and our ability to grow and acquire new work. In a number of published speeches and articles, union officers and organizers told employees in our competitors' shops how they were going to organize Donnelley, which had been growing, at times at the expense of union shops. Many Donnelley employees, understandably and logically, came to the conclusion that the union organizers who rang their doorbells at night were not really there to help them but were primarily interested in hurting Donnelley and, thereby, protecting union members in our competitors' businesses.

Secondly, I firmly believe that, in general, we have good, friendly, cooperative working relationships within our plants. This is not to say we are perfect; we are a long way from perfect. But I think most Donnelley employees understand that they have a lot more to lose than gain from union membership. Certainly one of the most satisfying aspects of my time in the Company has been the way in which our competitive success has permitted us to provide the kind of job security, job opportunity, safety, wages, and benefits outlined in this chapter. It is my earnest hope and sincere belief that Donnelley employees do indeed understand the great stake they have in helping to preserve the open shop. It has brought us a long way in the past and, in my opinion, is also the key to the future.

* * *

It must be apparent by now why this book begins with our commitment to our people. Since the beginning of our Company, our employees have been the key to our reputation as a printer, our character as a business firm, and our potential as an industry leader. My grandfather believed this. My father and his brother acted upon this conviction. And this living, real commitment has always been a source of much pride to me and my associates.

Even more important than our Company having this commitment is the fact that our day-by-day relations within Donnelley prove this commitment to our people and prompt them to respond with a similar commitment of their own. The result, of course, is the kind of teamwork we have here—teamwork that has made us grow in size and in stature to leadership in our industry.

People have told me that our kind of commitment to each other is increasingly rare in the business world. If so, this is tragic, as a lack of commitment to each other can only diminish the quality of the product, the service, the growth, and prosperity of a company and its people. To the extent this lack of commitment to each other exists elsewhere in our own industry, it is devastating, for the lack robs the printer of his feeling that his is a great vocation.

It is my firm belief that through growth and change and time Our Commitment to Each Other at Donnelley remains essentially unchanged. Certainly in my working career nothing has been as important to the operation of the Company, and nothing has been as satisfying to me personally, as the relationships I have enjoyed with the thousands of people with whom I have shared a mutual commitment.

CHAPTER TWO

Our Commitment to Others Outside the Company

Our second commitment, to others outside our Company, is very much like the first commitment —a two-way street. We do not live and operate in a vacuum, but depend for our well-being upon thousands of others—people, companies, and institutions of all kinds. These include the publishers who are our customers, the suppliers who provide us with buildings, equipment and printing materials, and the communities in which we operate and in which our employees live. We try to know them better so that we can be more effective, and encourage them to know us better and realize that our commitments are real.

Reuben Hamilton Donnelley   1864–1929

Our Customers

In a service-oriented business such as ours, customers play a particularly significant and important role. That's where the action really begins. Our services for them often form an almost integral part of their own operations, and we might be looked upon as another department of theirs, or an extension of their own organization. In fact, in the past many publishers, merchandisers, and other institutions operated printing departments themselves. Of late, the number has decreased markedly, in part because good customer management realized that printing was quite a different kind of business from theirs, requiring different and special talents. Publishers also have found it difficult to maintain the high activity necessary for economical operation.

My grandfather, who came to Chicago in 1864 to be the printing partner of a religious publishing firm that had printing facilities, learned this fact the hard way. As his publishing partners retired from the business, he tried to continue the publishing activities, which for decades handicapped the Company from realizing its full potential. There is, therefore, a sound, practical, as well as philosophical, basis for our Company's firm policy to stick to our own business and not to compete with our customers. As the printing business has grown more complex, this policy has become increasingly important, since it has enabled us to concentrate our full energies and resources on printing itself.

KNOWING THE CUSTOMER'S NEEDS

In supplying an important service, we have an obligation to learn everything we can about our customers' needs and problems of the present, plus plans and goals of the future. The good Donnelley sales representative becomes an expert at learning and analyzing his customer's needs. He seeks out the key people in the customer's organization. He asks penetrating questions. He listens more than he talks and he probes for the facts in depth. Finally, everyone handling a job must determine just what the customer has in mind.

The purpose of such research is to make it possible for us to tailor our efforts and methods to satisfy to the best of our ability the requirements of a given job for a given customer—so we can produce that true value the customer is seeking and deserves. Each customer is different and each job we do for him differs also in varying degrees. We must know these differences, respect them, and work them into an efficient method of production.

This doesn't mean that we shouldn't question the customer's concept of his requirements, and we often do. Sometimes the customer may not foresee the consequences of his plan—the extra costs or other disadvantages. We have an obligation to point out costs in dollars (not in generalities) and to suggest more economical or practical alternatives if they are available. With all the facts in hand, the customer can then decide how he wants to spend his money. We have a further obligation to be creative, to introduce new ideas on our own initiative, and not just to react to a customer's question or inquiry. An excellent example is our pioneering work in the development of heat-set printing in the 1930s. This work was not done at a customer's request, but was begun and carried through at our own initiative, and presented to our customers as an accomplished fact from which they could benefit. The development of our modular plants, designed for a single product, is another instance of a major improvement in printing production which resulted from our own creativity, not a mere reaction to prodding from outside.

Keep in mind also that a customer's needs change. The smooth routine that served the past may no longer suffice. We have the obligation to be flexible—to face tomorrow's plans with new methods, new procedures, new techniques. Our customers expect us to be forward looking, to grow with them, to accommodate their expanded needs. We have had great success in doing this even when it required the purchase of additional equipment, the training of new employees, the building of additional space, the expenditure sometimes of millions of dollars. We are committed to the printing business and, fortunately, have the financial strength to provide for our customers' growth requirements.

One of the most important responsibilities of a good sales representative is communications back-and-forth, either through him, or directly to others in our organization. In the initial stages, estimators, planners, engineers, buyers, designers, credit, and personnel executives may be involved, as well as sales, manufacturing, and general management. All the ideas and know-how of many experienced people are brought together to provide the best possible proposal for the salesman to present to the customer. Even so, many revised proposals may follow in succession.

Some customers wonder why we go to such lengths in drawing up contracts with detailed specifications and lengthy price schedules. It is our experience that it is best to work out as many details and provide for as many contingencies as possible in advance to avoid future misunderstandings and to form a basis for the many changes that usually develop. In fact, these negotiations further mutual understanding a great deal. The printer-customer relationship is a dynamic one, ever changing. On a long-term contract, changes can reach a significant number to accommodate a customer's changing requirements. In one case I remember, changes numbers one through five were agreed upon even before the main contract was signed! In some cases an understanding is reached between a customer and our salesman and implemented before it can be reduced to writing.

In working with customers, the really professional printing salesman thinks of himself not so much as a salesman, not as someone who receives invitations to bid and duly submits a price, but rather as a kind of business partner working to understand and fill the publisher's needs. He thinks in terms of total value encompassing design, quality, price, schedule, service—all of the very complex factors that add up to value.

Sometimes, of course, the publisher's value concepts may be limited by his own policies. Pricing standards, editorial standards, and union label requirements are examples of customer policies that sometimes affect our ability to work with publishers. Since each of these subjects can have a very substantial impact on our customer relationships, it seems appropriate to deal with each in some detail.

A FEW THOUGHTS ON PRICING

While buyers of printing are usually concerned with quality, service, and reliability, price is also a prime consideration. Our pricing policies and methods have evolved through many years. It is said my grandfather could hold a book in his hand and quote a realistic price for a reprint, or for a similar original publication. Now we detail each operation, with hour rates and speeds based on experience or careful engineering and accounting studies, or a combination of these. We expect to make a profit on every job we produce, and so provide the return on our high capital investment that is due our shareholders and is essential to our ability to survive, grow, and take care of our customers' ever changing needs.

However, our goal is to provide real value, which differs from customer to customer and may or may not be the cheapest price available anywhere. It is more than just ink on paper, bound in some fashion or other. There is real value in reliability and assured production under our Open Shop and in the dedication of thousands of Donnelley people to getting the job out on schedule. Quality is a prime objective of the salesman, customer representative, craftsman, quality expert and inspector, management at all levels; in fact, everyone in the Company can contribute to this value. The expertise of all is at the service of our customers, who come to rely on what we have to offer. Our modern facilities, technology, and high productivity tend to keep our prices reasonable, and so our customers also benefit from increased productivity, advanced technology, and other improved methods as they become available.

Nevertheless, customers sometimes show a tendency to buy on the basis of price only, without realistically evaluating our competitors' ability to produce at the quoted price.

This problem can take at least four forms, the first of which was put to me very pungently by an old printer from another company when I first became active in trade association work. "The way to make money in printing," he said, "is to load on the extras, and charge an hour of time for every tenth you actually put in." Unfortunately, the practice of quoting an unreasonably low price, with the expectation of "making it up on the extras," is still not unknown in our industry.

The second example is a larger-scale, longer-term, variant on the first. In cases in which the account is very large, involving a long-term contract and a heavy investment in equipment, the printer may again quote an unreasonably low price to get the contract. His assumption here is that once the publisher is committed the publisher will be forced to make upward adjustments in price, having no other realistic options.

The third situation we have found troublesome is that of a competitor who offers an inordinately low price in all honesty, because he simply does not understand the job on which he is bidding well enough to know what his costs will be. When he belatedly discovers that he cannot manage the job at the contracted price level, his customer is left with the disagreeable alternative of paying more or making a difficult, and perhaps costly, last minute decision to move to another printer.

Finally, we encounter cases in which the printer is also honest, with no intention of loading on extras or of seeking a price increase when the customer has no realistic alternative. He also is well aware of his costs, and still offers a bid so low that he cannot possibly show a profit. In these circumstances, the printer is either trying to buy his way into a new market or has excessive idle capacity and postpones the inevitable by seeking work at prices which cover only his out-of-pocket costs. If he persists, the inevitable is bankruptcy.

Our own approach is to develop sound cost standards and provide firm price estimates whenever possible, thereby minimizing cost-plus operations which provide so little protection for the customer.

Buyers whose main thrust is to shop around continually for the lowest possible price, regardless of other considerations, are not likely to develop the long-term, close, mutually advantageous relationships that have been the basis of success and growth for both our customers and our Company.

In the past especially, printers often extended credit terms more generous than warranted, frequently to their sorrow. It never seemed fair to ask those who paid their bills promptly to bear any significant share of costs resulting from those who didn't. I was not at all ashamed to read recently in the *Wall Street Journal* that we were among five of the Fortune 500 who had the lowest reserve for bad debts in proportion to accounts receivable. It says a lot about the financial strength and integrity of our customers.

EDITORIAL STANDARDS

Over the years we have consistently resisted the temptation to take on work we have judged inconsistent with the standards and image of our Company and offensive to the sensibilities of our employees. We do not accept just any sort of printing job for the sake of the sale, and we do not serve publishers whose only standards are profitability. For this reason we have on many occasions refused to bid on work of publishers who are known to deal in pornographic or semi-pornographic materials.

This does not mean that we never have a problem. We all know that legal and social standards have been changing.

What is pornographic; what can be carried in the mails; what can be shown in the theater; what can be sold on the magazine stands? Each new attempt of the Supreme Court to act and define standards in these areas seems only to set off new waves of confusion.

I personally think the courts have gone too far in creating a permissive society. But this is only one man's opinion. The main point is that opinions differ, and the question of what is in good taste and what is in bad taste is difficult to answer.

From a practical point of view we must recognize that it would not be possible for us to act as a censor on each and every piece of editorial material submitted to us. Although we may occasionally raise questions of taste with publishers, we simply are not in a position to review and pass judgment on each and every word, picture, and drawing. Furthermore, as a matter of trade practice, publishers rather understandingly are not willing to sign printing contracts conferring censorship authority on the printer.

Since individual censorship is not practical, our basic approach is to enter into contracts only with reputable publishers and then rely on them to stay within the bounds of good taste. If the publisher begins to drift beyond the boundaries of good taste we can discuss the matter. On several occasions we have done this, but generally speaking we have not had much of a problem.

Our primary reliance on reputable publishers to control editorial content is yet another reason why I am particularly proud that so many of America's finest publishers have elected to have their work done at Donnelley.

A FEW THOUGHTS ON THE UNION LABEL QUESTION

From time to time printing buyers have denied us the opportunity to bid on printing because our products do not contain a union label, more commonly known as the "union bug." This is a small buggish-looking mark, which a printing union or group of printing unions authorizes the printer to place on his product to indicate that no one other than union members has worked on that product in operations where those unions claim jurisdiction.

Printing buyers who require the union label are discriminating against open shop printers in favor of employers who have union shop contracts. It is as simple as that. These employers receive an economic reward for having union shop contracts, while employers whose employees have chosen not to elect a union are arbitrarily denied the opportunity to bid on the work. When our national labor laws very specifically indicate that employees shall be protected in their right not to join unions, it seems strange indeed for private buyers of printing to exercise a kind of economic coercion against open shop employees. Fortunately, the use of a union label buying policy is becoming increasingly rare.

Over the years this kind of buying policy has been little more than a nuisance for us at Donnelley. Virtually no commercial publishers who buy printing practice this kind of discrimination. In some cases where unions have tried to pressure them, these publishers have been offended by the rank discrimination inherent in such a buying policy. More frequently, however, the publisher is simply and totally concerned with buying his printing on the basis of quality, price, service, and other meaningful value considerations.

Actually, as I look back over the years, it seems quite possible that union pressures to get publishers to specify the union label have probably worked to our advantage. Faced with this kind of pressure more than one major customer has taken a good look at the question and has responded by telling us how proud he is to be doing business with us. They are impressed by a company in which the employee relationships are sufficiently good that employees do not feel it necessary to bring in outside union people to represent them and where the people are working closely together to produce a fine product. Essentially, they see our open shop as a badge of success and recognize the values it brings to them in terms of fine, dedicated people, good work practices, and assured production.

The one area where the union label buying policy occasionally does cause us a little trouble is in bidding on government printing. A number of government agencies (state buying authorities, school boards, and other governmental purchasing units) are under continuing union pressure to limit bidding to union label printers. Where unions gain strong political position they frequently push hard for a union label policy. They do this in spite of the fact that courts time and again have held that such policies, when practiced by the government, are clearly illegal. These court decisions have held that the union label requirement is against public policy, violates the equal protection and due process provisions of the United States Constitution, violates similar provisions in various state laws and constitutions, and, since it eliminates competition and facilitates monopoly, is prohibited by various anti-trust and other laws prohibiting restrictive trade practices.

An interesting example of the union label monopoly game at work occurred several years ago when we were awarded a contract to produce the original document of a new constitution for the State of Illinois, as proposed by the Constitutional Convention. On a Tuesday, with the Convention winding up many months of work and planning to sign the new Constitution on Thursday, with the type already set in Donnelley composing rooms and final printing set for

Wednesday, union officials initiated a three-hour filibuster to force the printing into a union shop. In that case we lost a very small piece of business. Although sad in some respects, the case was somewhat amusing in that we had obtained a very special kind of paper to facilitate maximum preservation of this historic document and, had we wanted to play games, could have thrown the Convention's closing schedule into chaos simply by holding onto the paper. I admit to some temptation, but we took a bigger view and, of course, released the paper.

When asked why he had picked Donnelley to do the work, the chairman of the committee charged with placing the printing said simply that Donnelley had been selected as the best for the job.

In the last analysis, I think this simple test, "best for the job," ought to be the key factor in selecting a printer.

SOME VALUED RELATIONSHIPS

We do have a long list of fine customers, whom we are proud to serve, and with whom we have had such fine relationships, some going back many decades. There is one periodical of high quality which we have been producing for seventy years. This category of our business has become a very large one, with magazines of all sizes and kinds, directed to many different audiences. Because he says eloquently so many significant things about salesmanship, business leadership, and indirectly our Company, I want to quote from a speech by the late Henry Luce before the Graphic Arts Council of Chicago in 1964, referring to the period when we really began our rapid growth in this field:

"My most intimate and memorable connection with the printing industry goes back a long ways," Mr. Luce said. "In 1927, *Time* was being edited and published in Cleveland. It was a very little magazine—hardly more than a 32-page self-cover job, strictly black and white, of course, and with a circulation of perhaps 100,000. We began to think that it might be possible to split our operation—to edit in New York and print in Chicago. The next thing I knew, a very distinguished gentleman, Mr. T. E. Donnelley, was knocking at the door of our very undistinguished offices. Over a period of six or eight weeks, Mr. Donnelley spent many days and nights in Cleveland, working with me on the minute details of a contract. The contract couldn't have been worth much to him and I was a very penny-pinching bargainer—yet, Mr. Donnelley treated the contract—and me—as if it were the biggest deal of the century. Well, it did turn out to be something of the sort—one of the world's biggest and longest-playing printing contracts.

"T. E. Donnelley was a terrific salesman—not in the sense of blandishment but in his tireless concern for the needs and wants of the customer, however small—and however aggravating, as I surely was. No man can ever get so big and important that he can afford to quit selling. Salesmanship is what a great deal of human life is all about—whether we are trying to persuade people of some lofty ideal of truth, or just peddling our wares.

"But it does make a difference whether our wares are good and whether we deeply believe in them. Ted Donnelley was devoted to printing. He was devoted to his own business, but he also saw his own business as part of the greatest civilizing instrument of mankind. Here is a shining example of Alfred Whitehead's famous dictum that 'A great society is a society in which its men of business think greatly of their function.' "

It is not very surprising that Harry Luce and father became fast friends. I had the good fortune, as a young printer, to be a beneficiary of that warm relationship, because Harry Luce was always very friendly to me.

The challenges of higher standards of quality, ever more exacting schedules, increased productivity, and sudden editorial changes in periodicals have been great since that time, but these bind us even more strongly to our chosen vocation.

OTHER PRODUCTS

Books are a category of our business that might be said to go back before the founding of the Company, for our Memorial Library in Chicago contains volumes produced by R. R. Donnelley in Canada before he came to Chicago in 1864. Encyclopedias have long been an important part of our business, as have been Bibles and other religious printing. Since the 1930s, elementary and high school texts have grown manyfold. After World War II, we entered the book club field, and recently we have expanded into trade and college textbooks. An aggressive program of mechanization and methods improvement has kept printing costs reasonably in line even in these highly inflationary times.

Our history of catalog production goes back to before the turn of the century. Now, with the closely related gravure tabloids, catalogs have become a major category. If merchandise is to sell, faithful reproduction is a must, a constant challenge. If the catalog does not reach the potential buyer on time, days of sales are lost which are never made up. Our obligation here is very clear.

Probably one of the most exacting parts of our business falls in serving the financial and legal printing markets. Here we face the challenge of many corrections and absolute accuracy in the shortest possible span of time with most of the work done in the late night and early hours of the morning. As I look back over the years, I take some personal satisfaction that I made the first customer contact and was the first service representative in this aspect of our business, which is now produced in two of our divisions, supported by a Financial Service Center facility in the New York Financial District.

Our Company is undoubtedly the largest printer of telephone directories in the world. In composition, accuracy is the prime requirement; in printing, legibility; in binding, durability; in all three, fast schedules and reasonable costs. We first printed the Chicago Telephone Directory in 1886, and have been doing it ever since. I would like to quote some recent remarks of John D. deButts, Chairman of AT&T, our largest customer in this field, at the dedication of a new directory facility. Referring to the printing of that first directory, Mr. deButts said:

"That was only ten years after the telephone was invented in 1876, and it was only one year after the American Telephone Company was incorporated, and they've been printing telephone directories ever since in increasing numbers. And they've been doing it for one reason, because the Donnelley Company and the Bell System have exactly the same credo, the best possible service or product at the least possible cost to the consumer, consistent with financial safety. And that's why these two great companies, I would say, have had such tremendous relationships over the years, because we respect each other as business people and as customer, and each serves the other well. Now, you add to that something that you don't always find between customers and client, and that is the greatest relationship on a friendly basis, a friendship, man to man, person to person, basis that exists between those in the Donnelley outfit and those in the Bell System. This is something that I had never experienced before in my life, and it is indeed a real pleasure as individuals, as well as a real pleasure from a business standpoint, to operate with R. R. Donnelley & Sons Company."

The last part of this preceding quote points up an aspect of our business that has been particularly rewarding to me and many of my associates. I have said we have fine customers, and it should be no surprise that fine companies tend to be made up of fine people. It is difficult to separate the two in one's own mind. When I recall and recount to my younger associates the truly wonderful friendships that have developed from the business over the years, I emphatically point out that we do not do business on friendship alone, but that if there is a sound economic basis, then friendly relations can further the interests of both sides, and become the frosting on the cake. We think it's a responsibility of general management to maintain cordial relations with their opposite numbers to enhance customers' confidence, to be available when needed, and to support but not interfere with normal salesman/buyer relations.

WORKING WITH THE CUSTOMER DURING PRODUCTION

Once the job is sold and the contract signed, many of the people mentioned earlier in this chapter shift to the execution phase. In addition, a Donnelley innovation, the customer service representative, comes into the picture to take prime responsibility for the job. He receives instructions, copy, dummies, layouts, etc. from the salesman, or directly from the customer, and becomes the prime contact with the latter, for he is always in the plant. He will write manufacturing and shipping instructions, requisitions for materials to the Purchasing

Department, request a final production schedule from the Planning Department, and follow the job to assure conformity to specifications, maintenance of quality standards, and adherence to schedules. The point is that he is in the plant on top of the job, the liaison with the customer, keeping informed, as necessary, both the customer and the salesman, who hopefully is spending a good part of his time selling more printing.

While the salesmen and customer service representatives are well known to our customers, all through our Company we have dedicated craftsmen, skilled technicians, highly trained and capable specialists in every aspect of printing and binding and all the related sciences and arts, most of whom rarely have occasion to work directly with our customers. And yet our customers know that these people are there. They know it through our salesmen, who regard all of Donnelley's people *and* their skills as part of the total package they have to sell. To some extent, our customers see the ingenuity and dedication of these many people in the work Donnelley produces, but the finest product rarely reveals all the work that went into it.

As our relationships develop in time, our goal is to establish, on the part of the customers, a feeling of confidence in the thousands of Donnelley people, equal to that in his own people, confidence that there is a real basis for our claim of a high degree of skill, motivations, and dedication.

Our customers must also feel confidence in the security of Donnelley operations. On more than one occasion, we have had a book or magazine customer who has entrusted to us highly confidential material in instances in which a premature leak would have ruined publication plans. Year in and year out, the prices appearing in the mail order catalogs we print are of intense interest to that customer's competitors. The same thing is true, of course, of material which is devoted to detailed descriptions of forthcoming new automobiles. Financial printing is especially sensitive, with the investment of very large sums of money turning on the facts set forth in the prospectus for a new issue of stocks or bonds. A very colorful example of the importance of security in financial printing occurred in years past when the Ford Motor Company was still privately owned. As Ford began long-range preparations for going public, it entrusted our Company with the printing of an annual report. This was an elaborate, four-color document, filled with detailed, confidential information about every aspect of the company's operations. Only one hundred copies of this report were printed each year. They were hand delivered in Dearborn by a senior Donnelley sales representative. Only those absolutely essential to production ever saw copy or finished product. Even I, then President, never laid eyes on the job. All proofs and extra press sheets were personally destroyed by the customer service representative. (And I mean *all;* we were not even permitted to retain a proof as a basis for billing.) This is typical of the way that Donnelley has proved that our customers may rely completely on the security of our operations. That security depends not so much on the guards at our entrance and shipping docks as on the thorough understanding by each and every Donnelley person that what the customer has committed to us is an inviolable trust.

INDIVIDUAL ATTENTION

We are by far the largest printing firm in the United States. We have a number of large, long-term contracts, but this is not true of an important and ever-growing part of our business. As we continue to grow, we are acquiring more and more customers with more modest requirements in books, catalogs, magazines, and other kinds of printing. This kind of business we want very much, and are devoting considerable management, sales, engineering, planning, and manufacturing attention, as well as capital resources, to meet these opportunities. This is not entirely new, since we have always prided ourselves on our ability, especially through the service representative function, to handle the small job. To add one more quotation in this section, there is a letter in my files that I treasure deeply. It is from the late Paul M. Angle, then Director of the Chicago Historical Society. It's dated May 27, 1960:

Dear Gay:

.... For nearly thirty-five years, I have been doing business with The Lakeside Press. I remember no job that has amounted to more than $3,500, and I can think of quite a few that have been in the $200 range. (This leaves out our dealings with the Extra Bindery, from which we sometimes got a statement for $20 or $25.) In all this time I have known that any job I had, no matter how small, would receive every attention, and I have been aware that the technical resources of the company were as fully available as they would have been had I been an important customer.

Donnelley's ability to handle jobs like *Time*, *Life*, and the *National Geographic* is one mark of greatness. Equally significant, it seems to me, is the company's solicitude for the small customer.

Sincerely yours,
Paul

I am glad to say there are many more similar letters in our files, both of earlier and later dates. I must admit though that there are some of a different tone. We are humans, and do make mistakes, which we must humbly admit to, rather than try to justify. We try not to make mistakes in the first place; if they are made we correct them as quickly as we can, and we take every possible precaution to avoid them in the future.

CONTINUING COMMITMENT

Once the job is completed and shipped, our commitment does not end, for it must be billed carefully and ethically.

We expect to collect what we are entitled to and no more, based on our original estimates, and the work we actually performed. It is our goal to make sure there are no surprises on the customer's bill—that it turns out about as he expected. We take pains to spell out in great detail in our contracts the prices applicable to the work we have undertaken. Then at the time of billing, we show in equal detail the application of those prices.

Periodic review of a customer's bills by the Donnelley staff can lead to changes in the way copy is furnished, or in production methods—changes which save money. This is always good news for the customer and is tangible evidence that we have his welfare at heart.

In addition, an occasional spot audit by our Internal Auditing

Department is made to verify the accuracy of our billings and billing procedures. Further, some of our contracts provide for a review of our billing by an outside auditor at the customer's request.

Our customers have come to know the results that can come only from people who are truly devoted to serving their best interests. Most inspiring to me have been the reactions to emergencies, always positive, and often at great personal inconvenience and sacrifice. The tragic President Kennedy death required two changes to be made in *Life* after initial books were shipped. The Churchill funeral story in *Life*, complete with on-the-spot pictures from England, was in final magazines in a matter of hours.

I have referred earlier to the dedicated response of Donnelley people when blizzards paralyzed Chicago and Mattoon and a tornado struck Willard. All these examples were beyond the call of duty and the normal interest in paychecks, but proof of individual commitment to meeting our customers' needs.

Our commitment to our customers is a living thing. We pledge that we will strive to do their work to their satisfaction in every respect and particularly, in the value, service, and attention they receive, and to earn their confidence in our complete integrity. Such statements express our commitment in words, but we express it in action on the job by what we do, how we do it, and when we do it. We are committed to the long-term welfare of our customers. Their lives and fortunes and ours are entwined. They need us, and we most certainly need them. If we do our jobs properly, we will help our customers succeed and prosper. As this occurs, our Company and its people should prosper also.

Suppliers

While in the preceding section, I dealt, quite understandably, at some length with our commitment to our customers,
I do not want to underestimate the importance of our suppliers and
their many fine contributions to our success.

It does not suffice to say that we currently process each year
about 1,000,000 tons of paper, 115 million pounds of ink, 16,000 tons
of binder board, 10 million yards of binding cloth, and so forth. Even
our total purchases of over one-quarter billion dollars, which include
materials, services, construction, and equipment purchases, under-
states the true picture, since more than half of the paper we use is
furnished on consignment by our customers. These are large numbers, but it is the quality of the material, services, and equipment, on
time delivery, and reasonable prices that enable us in turn to serve
our customers as we should. Printers sometimes tend to forget that
their quality is significantly dependent on the quality of the materials they have to work with. It is the old story of not being able to
make a silk purse out of a sow's ear. Our suppliers are essential to our
existence and success.

A supplier to R. R. Donnelley & Sons Company must have
financial responsibility, adequate physical facilities, management
integrity, and production skill. His reputation in the industry and
his record of performance become important considerations in our
purchasing decisions. Suppliers' research and development contributions are actively sought and greatly appreciated. We fully recognize
that these R & D expenditures must be financed with profits from
sales, and we consider this in selection of our suppliers.

It is generally accepted that printing is still very much an art,
greatly dependent on innovative creativity. We keep ahead of our

69

competition by trying to be the first to develop a "new mousetrap." Many times all we have is the idea; we leave it up to our suppliers to turn the idea into a satisfactory product or piece of equipment. This often requires extensive investment and risk and may even result in a proprietary development. In such instances, we work hard to establish stable, long-term supply relationships, consistent with good competitive practices.

Our commitment to our suppliers is guided by the Golden Rule, to treat them fairly and with consideration, with the goal of establishing mutual trust. We expect good competitive prices, but realize our suppliers must make a profit to stay in business and grow to meet our needs and challenges. The kind of relationship we seek and enjoy, to do business on the basis of merit, has no room for practices formerly common in the printing industry, with special favors, gifts, and kickbacks to buyers and others. Old timers have told me that ink suppliers thought the best insurance that their ink would print well was a silver dollar in the bottom of the ink bucket for the pressman. While colorful, those days thankfully are gone forever.

As with customers, our policy is not to compete with our suppliers unless unusual circumstances warrant. We think they know more about their business than we do, but we work with them closely to give them the benefit of our ideas, experience, observations, and tests of their products. We expect them to reciprocate at times with that extra bit of effort that makes the difference between success and failure. One major exception occurred in the 1930s when what seemed to be a superior method of making colored inks was rejected by all ink companies. With our limited knowledge and experience, we pioneered with great success, and now flushed colors are one of the industry's standard methods of making colored ink. Even so, we limit the percentage of ink we produce to leave the ink companies with the incentive to serve us in the best possible manner.

Many of our suppliers have been with us for generations. They are progressive companies, growing with us, and helping us grow, and meeting positively the many challenges we present them. In turn, we work with them to establish the friendly, long-term, mutually advantageous relationships that will also contribute to their success.

Our Other Publics

Important as our commitments to our customers and suppliers are, the Company's responsibilities, and the commitments which follow, extend also to the communities in which we operate, to government, and to society in general. Yesterday, a good corporate citizen was a company that offered a good product or service at a fair price which resulted in a fair profit and provided stable employment at desirable jobs. All these things are still essential, but I think that additional obligations are now generally recognized. Certainly, they are with us.

CONCERN FOR OUR ENVIRONMENT

Consider, for example, the widespread concern with the quality of our environment, which has occupied increasing public attention in recent years. Donnelley has a deep and abiding commitment to our environment, which dates back at least to 1907, when my father was appointed by Mayor Busse to head the Chicago Smoke Abatement Commission. Woe unto the engineer in our boiler room if more than a wisp of smoke was emitted from our stacks! We have long been the industry leader in environmental preservation. The Company has had afterburner controls on all of its letterpress presses in Chicago since the late 1950s. Even prior to that time, in the '30s and '40s, we used water washers to reduce those emissions, although I think the result was probably more steam than control. In more recent years, we have had an extensive program of replacing older devices with the most modern afterburner systems on both letterpress and offset equipment, considerably increasing both our capital and operating costs. In 1969, we became the first Chicago printer to operate a solvent recovery system to control hydrocarbon emissions from our rotogravure operations. In 1971, we tripled the capacity of that system; recently, further extensive additions have been made. While control of water quality has not been a problem of the same magnitude as that of air, we have also taken the appropriate and costly steps necessary to prevent our damaging the water supply of our communities.

An outstanding example of our commitment in this area, and of the faith of our employees in this commitment, occurred several years ago when Old Saybrook, Connecticut, called a town meeting to determine whether the waste water discharged into a local creek by the Donnelley Plant was harmful to the fish. With unfailing commitment and an admirable sense of the dramatic, our Division Director arose, seized a container of the accused waste water, and drank from it. While such an act clearly goes beyond the responsibilities set out in his job description, it was most effective and, I am happy to note, the gentleman concerned survives to this day.

There are many kinds of pollution to be avoided, and one of them is esthetic. Good typographic design has long been a hallmark of our Company, but good design goes farther. Back in the 1890s, a bright young architect, Howard Van Doren Shaw, who was a college friend of father's, heard that the Company was contemplating a new building on Plymouth Court. He convinced father of the value of good architectural design for a manufacturing building, especially in our industry, but father doubted that grandfather would be persuaded. However, the two went to grandfather's office, and he heard them out. He accepted the concept with unexpected enthusiasm, and the Plymouth Court plant was the first of its distinct style in the Chicago area. It has recently been nominated for landmark designation. Later Mr. Shaw designed the Calumet Plant, but unfortunately died before construction was completed; the tower was designed by Charles Z. Klauder. While both plants could have been built more cheaply, they have been a source of pride and inspiration to many. The usual sort of plain, ugly, steel water tower would have served our manufacturing needs in Crawfordsville perfectly well, but we covered it with a Florentine tower of brick and masonry. In our newer divisions, our effort has been to build plants that are not only as efficient and productive as we could make them, but are also handsomely designed and attractively landscaped, so that they enhance their respective communities, not detract from them. There is no reason why a factory should not be beautiful as well as functional.

RESPONSIBILITY TO OUR COMMUNITIES

We have always felt a commitment to be a contributing part of the communities in which we live and work. This commitment has taken many forms in addition to our concern with environment.

For many years the Company has provided financial support to a broad range of public service activities. This support goes to a variety of social services, both through Community Funds or United Funds and directly. It extends to higher education, to health care, to cultural institutions, and to nonpartisan good government programs.

Perhaps more important than the Company's financial support has been the volunteer activity of Donnelley people. You will find them in all the Donnelley towns, giving of their time, effort, and money to their churches, to their schools, to United Funds, conservation activities, Junior Achievement, Scouting and Boys Clubs, settlement work, even volunteer fire departments. A really complete list would fill the rest of this book. This sort of unpaid, arduous work, done without interest in personal glory but only for the benefit of the communities in which we live, has always been, it seems to me, one of the great strengths of our country. Donnelley people have a long-standing and well-earned reputation for always doing more than their share. At the same time, they have exercised a sensible degree of restraint required to fulfill their responsibility both to their jobs and to their families.

RESPONSIBILITY TO INDUSTRY

We have felt, too, a commitment to do our part in the cooperative efforts of American industry, which has done so much to benefit all of us. Because of this conviction, our Company was a charter member of the National Industrial Conference Board and its YAMA conferences and of the Chicago Association of Commerce and Industry. My father was a founder of the Associated Employers of

Illinois and of the Employers' Association of Greater Chicago and was a founder and first chairman of the Taxpayer's Federation of Illinois. Today, the Company belongs to the two major national business organizations, to ten similar groups active on the state level, and to more than a dozen of a local nature. And we do not just "belong to" such groups. We work at it, providing board members, officers, specialized technical advisors, and other support on a very substantial scale.

This connection is especially apparent in our own industry, where we are active with manpower and money in the Printing Industries of America and in a half dozen of its local and regional affiliates, in The Book Manufacturers' Institute, in the Gravure Technical Association, and in the Graphic Arts Technical Foundation, including its National Scholarship Trust Fund. We do not always expect direct benefits to the Company from commitments of this kind. After all, our Company is well staffed, with our own experts in a great variety of fields. In part, we cooperate in these activities for the good of the entire industry. Our position is that, generally speaking, whatever helps the graphic arts industry in some way helps Donnelley.

It seems to me that activity of this kind also reflects our attitude toward our competitors. We have always been fiercely competitive but never, I think, unfairly so.

RESPONSIBILITY TO GOVERNMENT

Over many decades we have remained conscious of our commitment to government. While this commitment starts, I suppose, with such basic matters as paying our taxes and obeying the law, our responsibility is more extensive. Numerous Donnelley people have served and are serving in local governmental office, on school boards, on city councils, on planning commissions, and on a wide variety of advisory bodies.

It is a long-standing tradition in the Company that Donnelley people as individuals actively support political parties and their candidates for public office, both with money and with time. This kind of individual participation does much to make the two party system work. The Company, while carefully refraining from making financial contributions to candidates, has never hesitated to make its views on public issues known to local officials, members of state legislatures and of the Congress, and the leaders of the Executive Branches. Sometimes we think it more effective to do so as individuals, or as an individual Company; at other times we prefer to work with the associations to which we belong. I feel very strongly that, under our American system, this is not only our right but our responsibility. I am proud to say that in numerous instances of communicating our views over many years, I do not know of a single time we have urged an action that might have been helpful to the Company, in a short-term, narrow sense, but would have been generally damaging to a community, a state or to our nation.

* * *

The progress the Company has made over the years has been strongly influenced by our relationships and commitments to our various publics—publishers, suppliers, communities, government, and the public at large. Our ability to improve and grow—our ability to be a good printer—depends, in part, on the vitality and character of these closely related groups. We have worked hard to find and select outstanding publishers and excellent suppliers. We have exercised extreme care in selection of plant communities—and within them we have operated effectively and constructively, both with government at all levels and with the public in general. We have done all these things because we recognize our commitment to those outside the Company—and, as a result, I believe they as well as we have been strengthened by it.

CHAPTER THREE

Our Commitment to Excellence

Our third commitment is the natural result of our first two. Our ability to meet this commitment to excellence depends on the success of our relationships with each other and with our customers, suppliers, and the communities in which we operate. When these relationships are of high quality, our basic goal of excellence in every product, service, and facet of our business becomes obtainable. Indeed, given the proper tools, materials, and resources, it is the human being's attempt to achieve perfection that creates excellence—not only in printing but in all aspects of living.

Excellence in Donnelley printing means applying the finest technology and skill to produce the best work, for its purpose and at its price, that is available anywhere. Excellence at Donnelley also means meeting the challenges of change so that whatever the technology, methods, and skills of tomorrow, our ability to achieve excellence will continue.

77

Thomas Elliott Donnelley   1867–1955

Excellence

For a printing company to state that it is committed to excellence is a bold claim and not one to be made lightly. Every printer worthy of the name produces excellent work at times. Some do so frequently, some very seldom, but for Donnelley to claim that we are *committed* to excellence suggests that we produce excellent work *all* the time. Well, we wish, of course, that this were true. But when we say we have a Commitment to Excellence (as we have a Commitment to Each Other, to Others, and to Profit and Growth), this is not a boast. It is rather an identification of a very important Donnelley goal. We want every product and every service of ours to be of *exceptional merit*, to be *unusually* good, to be *consistently* better than anyone else can consistently produce. And we do everything we possibly can to insure that this goal will be achieved. Excellence is a very dynamic goal in the field of printing. What is excellent today may be only good or even second-rate tomorrow, because of the volatile state of today's printing technology.

Excellence in our products and services defies a short, pat definition because excellence—like integrity, honesty, and fairness—is an ideal which men strive to make a reality. To understand and define our commitment to excellence, it is useful to look at the nature of excellence in printing, the roots of our commitment, and finally, how we achieve excellence, nurture a climate to stimulate creative effort, and maintain excellence in an everchanging world.

THE NATURE OF EXCELLENCE

Excellence in printing results from combining good materials with good artistic design, superior craftsmanship, and careful handling by dedicated people in every phase of the services we offer

81

customers. Excellence in printing is the finest possible presentation of words, art, and pictures so that the exact message of the author, artist, or photographer is readily and effectively conveyed to the reader. The presentation of the printed word must be so pleasing to the eye that the reader is unaware of type, spacing, and design. On the other hand, in printing pictures, drawings, and other artwork, we strive for absolutely faithful reproductions that quicken the reader's awareness of their fidelity and inherent beauty.

In fact, excellence in the final product is achieved only by excellence in every phase of the printing process: clean, artistically-designed type, properly spaced; faithful reproduction in all other preliminary operations; carefully-prepared plates, precise in every dimension and detail; paper of strength, consistency, and finish appropriate to the job; inks, scientifically mixed, smoothly applied, and chemically prepared for proper trapping; presswork, combining craftsmanship with materials to produce clear, crisp, beautifully-printed pages; and binding, with products precisely folded, trimmed, and bound to last within the parameters of anticipated use.

Benjamin Franklin, patron saint of printers, expressed his views by saying that he "always liked a form well planed down, being adverse to those overbearing letters that hold their heads so high as to hinder their neighbors from appearing." In terms of overall excellence, he said that printing should be "readable rather than eccentric, plain rather than decorative, tasteful rather than unique and useful rather than useless." These expressions are as fresh, accurate, and relevant today as they were some 200 years ago. Excellence in printing involves more than quality manufacturing. Our sales people; our personnel in customer service, inspection, material handling; our engineers; our staff specialists; and all in staff support areas play distinct roles in achieving our commitment to excellence.

THE ROOTS OF OUR COMMITMENT

Our commitment to excellence is rooted in our heritage. I have suggested that excellence is the result of man's attempt at perfection, which certainly was a motivating force for our founder, Richard Robert Donnelley. Some of the books he produced before coming to

Chicago are in our Memorial Library and attest to his early mastery of the canons of good bookmaking. Not only was he a top compositor himself, but he knew what was required in woodcuts and engravings, and how to obtain the finest results in his pressroom and binderies. He formulated and handed down high standards of excellence that guide us even to this day.

Just as our present commitment to excellence is total, and not limited to manufacturing, our founder sought excellence beyond printing production itself. He was aware of what the best printers across the land were doing and was a great admirer of such outstanding leaders as De Vinne and Updike. In fact, our trade name, "The Lakeside Press," was inspired as much by R. R. Donnelley's high regard for the Riverside Press, an eastern printer of the highest quality and reputation, as it was by our location near Lake Michigan.

He felt the need for a pressmark, and, in 1897, J. C. Leyendecker designed the first "Donnelley Indian." The Indian's head was silhouetted against a blockhouse on the shores of Lake Michigan—thus associating The Lakeside Press with frontier life and midwestern development. The design of the Indian has changed over the years, just as printing technology has, but the pressmark remains a symbol of our commitment to excellence.

In 1871, when grandfather built the Lakeside Building on the southwest corner of Clark and Adams Streets, he clearly recognized a close relation between well-designed, high-quality buildings and the continuing production of well-designed, high-quality printing. Intended as a center in the Midwest for printing and publishing, the building's architecture represented one of the first attempts to introduce Gothic design into commercial and office buildings. Until the advent of the skyscraper, it was considered high on the list of Chicago's carefully designed buildings.

I have mentioned R. R. Donnelley's acceptance of architect Howard Van Doren Shaw's concept that a factory did not have to be ugly, but should in fact be well designed, without extravagance, to reflect the high character of its use. Almost eighty years later, though no longer owned by us, Shaw's Plymouth Court building stands handsome, yet functional.

In the early 1900s, as our business grew, T. E. Donnelley emphatically said, "I want a building that will reflect that the printing business is an art as well as a science." Of the Calumet Plant, father later wrote, "We have tried to make the architecture of the Calumet Avenue building typical of the spirit of The Lakeside Press—substantial in its solidity, honest in its purpose, and beautiful in its restrained dignity. To my knowledge, there is no building in the country built for printers which has been built for greater permanence, and it expresses the faith of the management that those who take up the work after us will, from generation to generation, maintain its preeminence in the printing arts."

Completed in 1929, the Calumet Plant still proclaims—inside and outside—its character and dignity; and the hum of the presses still proclaims fine printers at work. Our continuing reverence for great printers over the centuries is evidenced by the many printer's marks on the outside of the plant, in the leaded glass windows of the Memorial Library, and elsewhere. The plant's imposing entrance, the fine wood and glass partitions of many offices, the beauty of the Gothic hallway leading from the eighth-floor galleries to the Memorial Library remain. Inside the two-story library, which was conceived by Reuben H. Donnelley and Thomas E. Donnelley as a memorial to their father and now is considered a memorial to all three, are leaded windows, carved bookcases, a massive stone mantel, and some of grandmother's best furniture. The bookcases are filled with products we have created over the years. Often described as beautiful, it is more than a memorial. Today, we receive friends and customers, conduct managers' meetings, and celebrate employee service anniversaries and retirements in the library.

Our founder's request for excellence was carried forth by Thomas E. Donnelley. In the 1920s, the Extra Bindery was established to restore and hand-bind books by centuries-old methods. It served as an inspiration to modern bookbinders and as a standard against which machine bookbinding could be compared. Called Graphic Conservation today, the department continues to rebind and restore old books, plus many manuscripts and works of art—commissions obtained because of its reputation for excellence.

At Christmas 1975, the seventy-second edition of *The Lakeside Classics* was distributed to our employees, retired employees, and friends. It is our only publishing activity other than our annual report and company magazine. This series started in 1903 as an appropriate Yuletide greeting and as an example of how a fine book in convenient format could be produced by craftsmen and more experienced apprentices using regular production methods.

The original format reflected the then current custom of gentlemen carrying books in their pockets. The size has not changed over the years but every twenty-five years the format is adjusted to reflect advances in manufacture and changing concepts of design. *The Lakeside Classics* have received worldwide acclaim for their quality, format, editorial excellence, and contributions to scholarship.

Beyond these outward signs that survive to this day as reminders of our heritage and as evidence of how our commitment to excellence developed in many aspects over the years, it seems fair to conclude that our forebears created a spirit and an atmosphere that must have stimulated those about them and those who followed to reach for higher and higher standards.

HOW IS EXCELLENCE ACHIEVED

The inextricable interweaving of all our commitments charts an obvious path to excellence.

In each of our product areas, we number the finest publishers among our customers. Our suppliers, many of years' standing with us, work with us so that we have the best in buildings, equipment, and materials—not only today, but tomorrow. Lastly, we have what 112 years of doing business have proved to be the most important of all ingredients: our own people. In the last analysis excellence must be achieved by people, by a combination of their efforts, their standards, and their contributions all brought together in a climate of excellence.

We have many veteran craftsmen in Chicago and Crawfordsville whose careers have been influenced directly, or by second generation knowledge, by our founder, by T. E. Donnelley, and by colleagues who built the strong foundation of our business. Many veteran craftsmen have moved to new divisions where they have transferred their knowledge and skills to people of varying backgrounds and cultures. In this way, the people in our newer divisions also come to understand and assume our commitment to excellence.

And, once the newcomers are part of the Donnelley team, their innate talents have room to expand, to refine—often beyond their own expectations. They find it easy to fit into the climate of excellence because concepts like teamwork, Open Door, Open Shop and one-to-one relationships are not only policies but a way of life in our day-by-day practices.

A CLIMATE OF EXCELLENCE

But how does one create a climate of excellence? It is one thing to establish and define a standard; it is quite another to create an atmosphere that will inspire and stimulate fine people to do the countless things that are all part of striving for perfection. But, just as many grains of sand make up the desert, we do many day-by-day things to create a climate of excellence. Things already mentioned —our building, the Memorial Library, our proud trademark, the Graphic Conservation Department, *The Lakeside Classics*—all play a part in creating an atmosphere within which we all work.

It is interesting to note how our efforts to create and maintain this climate have continued through good times and bad.

During the Great Depression of the 1930s, a group of craftsmen and others from our Chicago offices formed the Holiday Press, which was devoted to publishing and printing the finest in books. The Company contributed the use of our equipment and the employees contributed their evenings and Saturdays and a few dollars for materials. The pace was leisurely but the rewards were five or six copies of a gem of a book—plus a gala publishing celebration attended by these printers, the authors, and the illustrators.

Few of us will forget Carl Sandburg with his guitar at the old Brevoort, or the reminiscences of George Ade at his Indiana farm, which included a private nine-hole golf course. (Not all the Holiday Press members' skill on the links matched that of their craft.)

From 1930 to 1952 and again starting in 1974, the eighth-floor galleries of our Calumet Plant have seen more than seventy-five exhibitions of a wide range of the graphic arts, fine art showings, including old masters as well as Grant Wood and Thomas Benton, who appeared at the opening of their shows, and an exhibition at the end of 1975 of the arts and crafts created by people from every division and sales office of our Company.

In more recent years, we have cooperated to bring to Donnelley a replica of the Trajan letters, a classic design of Roman letters surviving today on Trajan's Column erected in Rome in A.D. 113. Because these designs survive as an ideal for all western lettering, our replica, the finest in existence, hangs today in our exhibition hall as a continuing reminder of the high standards for which we reach.

Our advertising department creates a wide range of ads, prints, and direct mailing pieces, all carefully prepared to define our standards and achievements. These products are designed to create an understanding and impression of excellence, not only in buyers of printing, but also for all of us within the Company.

Thus, we do many things to create, to nourish, to perpetuate a climate of excellence.

In the 1940s this creative climate was beautifully described in a mailing about our Company's advertising philosophy. It was called "Jacob wrestled with an Angel" and explained the aims of our carefully crafted advertising pieces. The first aim, Advertising Manager Harry J. Owens wrote, ". . . is very much like that of all advertising. It is to draw favorable attention to this enterprise and its work.

"A second aim may be described as a special kind of sampling . . . to give [buyers of printing] glimpses . . . of what is possible with great freedom.

"A third objective of our advertising—a by-product valuable beyond the highest price you could name—is the powerful quality stimulus to our craftsmen that comes from frequent calls on them to produce printing that is, at least in some detail, a shade higher up the scale than anything they have attempted before.

"The production of a Donnelley advertising piece, in other words, provides something of an occasion for flexing the muscles of our craftsmanship—for stretching a little farther the length of our reach toward perfection. We try to fly as close to the sun as we can without letting it singe the feathers of our wings . . . .

"No absolutely perfect piece of printing has ever been done at The Lakeside Press. So far as we know, none has ever yet been done by anyone anywhere in the wide world. Perhaps none ever will be. Not absolutely perfect!

"But, as we see it, these facts do not . . . excuse us from struggling everlastingly toward the perfection we know from the beginning we can never quite attain. 'Ah, but a man's reach,' said Browning, 'should exceed his grasp, or what's heaven for?'

"In this urge toward perfection—this eternal quest for quality—even though we fail in part, yet we succeed in part. The veil is a little lifted; we catch the distant gleam of better and still better things. The craftsman who takes part in the battles on the heights will never again be quite as he was before. His eye will be a little clearer, his stature surely a trifle higher; and there will be new strength in him that will remain to the end of his days.

"Like Jacob in the old Bible story, he has wrestled with an angel all through the dark night; and if, like the old Israelite, he finds his thigh out of joint when daylight comes, he has not wholly lost the contest; for, like Jacob, he can say to the angel, 'I will not let thee go, except thou bless me.' "

We have made excellence an all-consuming objective permeating virtually everything we do. I am confident that we shall continue to find ways to foster and preserve this essential ingredient so important to our Company's success and to a daily, personal satisfaction realized by each of us.

MAINTAINING EXCELLENCE IN A CHANGING WORLD

Since excellence is not static, what is excellent today may be only good tomorrow—or even second-rate. So it is vital that we always look at ways to perpetuate it. There are many, and their kinds are as numerous as the people in our Company. The ways are diverse: an employee's suggestion—so simple it should have been self-evident—on a way to save materials, improve production, increase quality, or expedite shipments. A new method of billing that eliminates duplication and expedites the communication of data. Engineering new stackers to handle accelerated signature delivery on high-speed presses. Harnessing the laser for new refinements in four-color printing. Simple or complex, the result of a sudden inspiration or intensive research, the ways to new levels of excellence have one thing in common: they all meet the challenge of change.

During my working lifetime, the changes exacted by new technologies, new growth, and new communications demands—in all of industry, in printing and within our Company—have been remarkable. However, considering the caliber of our people, perhaps it is not remarkable that we all have shown excellent flexibility, willingness and ability to accommodate change.

Fifty years ago, most of the preliminary work of printing was accomplished by the skilled hands of craftsmen. Today, the never-ending inventiveness of the human mind has created new processes and equipment that have transferred the former skills in the craftsman's hands to the skills in the craftsman's brain. The very growth of our craft jobs from yesterday's handful to today's hundred-plus attests to the fact that craftsmen must cope with the advances of technology.

Hand in hand with technological progress has been the expansion of the printing industry. Population explosion, increased universal education, higher standards of living, new communications techniques, devices, and media have triggered a proliferation of transmitted knowledge and fostered new packages for the printed word. Encyclopedias are within the financial reach of the average family and important to the family's educational progress. Catalogs serve urban dwellers near stores—not just rural families miles from a retailer. Millions of directories go with telephones in almost every home. Magazines devoted to every conceivable subject and activity join the growing number of periodicals covering current events. Books to entertain, books to interpret trends, books on how to do anything from playing the stock market to building a better birdhouse vie for the reader's attention. More and more financial reports and prospectuses appear as businesses multiply and new industries are born of new technology and new needs for services.

To meet the mushrooming growth in printing quantity, quality, and diversity, we have made fundamental changes in our Company. Among the most significant things we have done to help us maintain excellence in a changing world is the development of modular plants and the formation of product-oriented groups that permit further specialization in marketing, production, and distribution. When I speak of modular plants I am referring to plants that are specially designed and equipped to produce one particular product. Every feature of the plant—the basic layout, the provisions for material flow, every piece of equipment—is targeted so that from the receipt of materials and the beginning of manufacturing to binding and shipping of the final product everything is carefully tailored to produce that product in the finest, most efficient way.

The modular concept, which most recently has created the short-run book module at Crawfordsville, was born in our Company with the building of Willard—a division originally devoted to producing telephone directory services. Warsaw was created to produce catalogs, Old Saybrook to print *Life*. The blossoming special interest magazine field fostered Glasgow.

Dwight and Lancaster West were planned for improved product-flow and materials handling innovations necessary for the mass movement of materials telephone directory manufacture necessitates. The quality produced by these divisions is an excellent example of how product specialization affords complete control over the manufacturing process from the receipt of paper to the final product. Modular organization also encourages specialization of equipment to a degree which would otherwise probably not occur.

Modular concept successes contributed to our decision to experiment with the group plan of sales and manufacturing. Tested with books, the group organization concentrates management skills and sales people on a line of products which are manufactured by divisions specializing in the product. When the group concept proved successful with books, three groups were formed—each with its own sales force and manufacturing divisions—for books, magazines, and catalogs/directories. As the markets for the third group expanded, we saw the need for separate groups for catalogs and directories and, in 1975, created the four groups which function more or less autonomously within our Company—in a fashion similar to Chevrolet, Buick, and other independent divisions within General Motors.

In back of the modular and group concepts lies the excellence that specialization nurtures. Within each product group we are able to associate marketing, engineering, and manufacturing skills from start to finish. All these people concentrate their energies on finding the best possible ways and doing the best possible job of producing a particular product. Specialization also permits greater and more effective materials inspection and quality control—two areas which have seen rapid growth in recent years. Made even more imperative by increasing competition and continuing inflation, materials inspection, and various quality control programs in our divisions—especially statistical quality control—these factors have reduced costs while increasing the excellence of our products.

Our acceleration of these programs has influenced our suppliers to look for new ways to improve materials and research new products to serve the printing industry. Indeed, we feel our stringent specifications have helped forward industry equipment and materials development over the years. Some of our testing and research, particularly with inks and papers, have provided the nucleus of new product lines for suppliers.

Because we are a service business rather than a company that creates and markets a product, our research efforts relate to the needs of our customers and usually have been linked with those of our suppliers. The multiplicity of the products we handle precludes the feasibility of laboratory research, which large food and car manufacturers, for example, conduct. The large number of small companies in the printing industry—as opposed to a few giants in the automotive industry, for example—makes scientific printing research more difficult. These factors have guided our research to improvement and adaptation rather than invention, although Donnelley inventions have included new designs such as those for stackers, stream feeders, and other innovations.

In our quest for new levels of excellence, continual search has been as important as research. Today, we look all over the world for technological genius and machinery that can improve our products.

For example, German creativity is as alive as ever and is producing press and preliminary area advances without parallel. The Japanese also are making important contributions to printing technology. In our search for new avenues of excellence, we have hired consultants, and we have acted as consultants to suppliers.

The point is there is no door we won't step through to discover new ways to make our excellence even better. Many changes offer new economies as well as additional quality. This is vital to growth because a seemingly endless wave of inflationary pressures has put a new spotlight on costs.

At Donnelley, however, we have always believed that quality never must be tarnished by the pressures of cost. An apparel manufacturer once said that no high fashion had ever been created that someone couldn't make cheaper—and worse. And that is what our commitment to excellence is all about. We are ever seeking new ways to cut costs, to improve service, to create savings—but never at the expense of quality.

Similarly, whatever changes invention and technology bring, the roots of our success will remain strong and will grow.

* * *

One of our long-time customers, the Bell Telephone System, has structured its fantastic growth and technological development on the rule that every new development must interface—must work—with the previous equipment.

In a way, that is our approach to change, too. However different the tools and techniques of our business will be in future years, the tools and techniques will still be used by our people, within the framework of team cooperation characterized by integrity, honesty, dedicated endeavor, and devotion to quality. These characteristics are priceless; yet they cost little because they are intrinsic in the kind of people we have, the kind of heritage we've been given and the kind of Company that together we have built.

CHAPTER FOUR

Our Commitment to Profit and Growth

Our last commitment, to profit and growth, is also so dependent upon our first three that it is not easy to think of it in isolation, nor to decide what best belongs in this chapter.

Profit and growth have a relationship of their own. A no-profit no-growth situation would presage the end of our successful enterprise, with incalculable harm to employees, customers, suppliers, and stockholders. A history of growth without profit would also be self-defeating.

On the other hand, adequate profits and return on investment are the basis for continued financial health and growth. Further growth can and should, if properly planned and executed, result in greater and sounder profits, as well as more security and opportunity for individuals, better services and values for customers, and a better investment for shareholders.

Elliott Donnelley   1903–1975

Profit and Growth

Our commitment to profit and growth is so intertwined with our other commitments, both strengthening them and drawing strength from them, that it is not easy to discuss as a separate topic. But it is a commitment of great importance, and, in speaking of it, I intend to touch on the early growth of the Company, our decentralization, and our organizational development, both with respect to staff functions, like engineering, and with regard to structural changes, such as our group organization. I also think it important to look at our financial resources and our financial controls, including such matters as dividend policy, sales forecasts, and budgeting. All these have been indispensable to the profitability of the Company and to its gratifyingly continued growth.

EARLY GROWTH

History does not record the total employment in 1864 of Church, Goodman and Donnelley, the publishing partnership formed upon R. R. Donnelley's arrival in Chicago; but it could have been not much more than a hundred or so. Later, during hard times, personnel dropped to a mere forty, and whether that included grandmother, who had to keep the books to save the cost of a bookkeeper, we do not know either. In later years, she reminisced about her personal and family sacrifices because the business needed a new press or some other equipment. She considered such suppliers diabolical in obsoleting present equipment, or guilty of shoddy workmanship, judging from the short-lived usefulness of the machine in question.

There were many financial difficulties and reorganizations over the early years, culminating in 1889 in the establishment of a creditors' committee to determine the future, if any, of R. R. Donnelley

97

& Sons Company. Fortunately, the large majority expressed confidence in the Company and its leadership, and both were given a reprieve and additional time to work off not inconsiderable debts. With the help of his sons, Reuben H. and Thomas E., who had just graduated from college, R. R. Donnelley accomplished this, and the long period of sustained growth and increasing profits was begun, to extend until this day. Our well-known conservative financial policy has a solid, long term, if somewhat painful, basis.

In the early years, as the publishing members of Church, Goodman and Donnelley moved into other fields, it did not take long for my grandfather to realize that a printer and a publisher needed quite different talents to succeed, and that he was primarily a printer. Even my grandmother's excellent *Lakeside Cookbook,* written "to help keep the presses busy," and many other publishing efforts of varying success could not maintain a viable publishing activity.

It was Thomas E. Donnelley's firm conviction that a publisher-printer would be constantly tempted to do something economically unsound in either of the two areas to benefit the other. His wisdom is supported by the fact that many publishing firms outside the newspaper field have dropped their production facilities, while only a small minority have retained theirs.

Father's conviction also has given us a guideline to our relationship to others and to our own growth: stay in the fields where our experience, knowledge, and special talents can offer a particularly useful and needed service. This has kept us out of the areas of activity of our customers on the one hand, and of our suppliers on the other, except in certain rather special circumstances. It is our belief that this policy has afforded us many advantages and helped avoid a number of pitfalls.

OUR ATTITUDE TOWARD ACQUISITIONS

I have often been asked by both our own people and others what plan we had for acquisitions, and, if we were so firmly committed to growth, why we had not made a number of them. We simply did not want to become a conglomerate moving into fields where we had no special talents to offer. Many acquisitions have been offered, but when we apply the same standards that we have for ourselves, or analyze their potential to meet such standards, few can measure up.

Many years ago, a good friend and owner of a printing company urged us to take over his business at a handsome price, based not on past or present profits, but his predictions of future potential profits, and he gave many reasons why they were assured. I had my doubts, and told him we had plenty of problems of our own to solve and could see no justification in paying him a goodly sum to take over his. It is not that we are against acquisitions. In fact, over the years we have investigated a number in depth, and hope we will find some with a good fit for us and also up to our admittedly high standards. Actually, there is responsibility definitely assigned for this function in general management.

On the other hand, we have been approached concerning a merger into a larger company. While there were some attractions to these proposals, we have always come to the conclusion that we would best serve the long-term interests of our customers, employees, and stockholders by remaining independent.

CONTINUED GROWTH

Because of our genuine dedication to integrity, quality, and service, more and more customers have entrusted their printing needs to our hands. Some contracts are long term, especially if a large investment in facilities is needed; others are short term or for a single job. The printing industry is characterized by a certain amount of turnover, but over the years we have managed to attract and hold more than we lost. Hence, with few interruptions, our growth has continued for over a century.

The business outgrew the Lakeside Building on Clark Street in the Loop, and in 1897 moved into the newly constructed building at the south end of Plymouth Court, which was doubled in size a few years later. In 1912, the first, small section of the Calumet Plant was completed to house the heavier equipment needed for efficient catalog and directory production. After World War I, that plant was expanded to approximately half its present size and was finished in 1929, when Plymouth Court was vacated and later sold. Expansion

continued through the purchase of vacant land and adjacent buildings, and construction of new ones, so that today we have almost
two million square feet for the Chicago Manufacturing and Electronic Graphics Divisions, and our Corporate Headquarters on the
Near South Side of Chicago.

DECENTRALIZATION AND ORGANIZATIONAL GROWTH

In 1921 we began our strategy of establishing manufacturing
facilities away from Chicago in communities of moderate size.

Chronologically:
Crawfordsville, Indiana
which has been expanded many times
Willard, Ohio, in 1956, followed in rapid order by
Warsaw, Indiana
Lancaster, Pennsylvania
Old Saybrook, Connecticut
Dwight and Mattoon, Illinois
Glasgow, Kentucky, and most recently
Elgin, Illinois, and
Gallatin, Tennessee

This dispersion has effected economies of concentration on similar
products, closer proximity to ultimate use, better plant layouts, and
less material handling, among other benefits. And, as we have grown
and become more and more of a national company, it has become
advantageous to have sales offices spanning the country and closer
to customers not located in the Midwest.

The growth of people in numbers and effectiveness has paralleled
and supported our physical growth, which could not have happened
without them. Obviously, more people working together need a more
fully developed organization to make their efforts fully effective and
productive. This naturally evolved to meet the changing needs over
our long period of growth. Earlier, all executive and administrative
functions could be carried out mainly by a small, closely knit group
of talented people. The best channel of communication was probably across the lunch table reserved daily in the corner of Harvey's

Restaurant in the old Dearborn Street Station across the street from our Polk Street Plant.

However, even from the beginning there was some division of labor and delegation of responsibility, both line and staff—bookkeeping first, and then salesmen. To allow the latter to concentrate on their selling efforts, various functions formerly handled by them were assigned to special units, such as estimating, purchasing, customer service (formerly called operating), planning and scheduling, billing and later design.

Both R. R. Donnelley and T. E. Donnelley had a keen interest in the technological improvement of equipment, processes, and materials. Their method was to consult with our suppliers, pass on their ideas, and inspire constant progress. After the turn of the century, Engineering became an important part of the organization, contributing significantly to our productivity, quality, and growth. Improved equipment design was its main responsibility, and it originated a number of concepts, usually developed in collaboration with our suppliers. By taking this lead, we could and can stay ahead of our competition in quality and productivity. Building layout and design is another engineering responsibility shared with architects and outside engineers. Engineering also has purview over building and equipment maintenance. In earlier days, the machine operator was expected to take care of most maintenance himself, but with present more sophisticated equipment, including electronic controls, fully equipped and staffed maintenance departments in each manufacturing division are needed to keep operations at peak efficiency and delays to a very minimum.

In the early 1900s, we were probably the first in our industry to apply the concepts of industrial engineering to printing. C. G. Littell, who later became President, had read an article about Frederick Taylor's pioneering work. He and father became so interested that they visited Taylor in his Pennsylvania home, and Mr. Littell stayed on for a series of lectures. Different operations were studied to eliminate useless or inefficient elements, establish the best methods, and then set soundly based time standards which could be attained by a competent worker without undue fatigue. This has been of inestimable value not only to manufacturing management, but also to provide the basis for accurate scheduling, cost estimating, and realistic pricing as well as to support billing for customers' work that had not been, or could not be, estimated in advance.

Research and Development was established formally in the 1930s when it became evident that chemists, physicists, and other scientists were needed to study and improve the many processes and materials involved in our business. Properly trained scientists with imagination and creativity were required to advance the technology of the graphic arts in such diverse fields as the study of light, the chemistry of color, adhesive formulations, paper, plating techniques, new printing surfaces, and photography. Today the list has grown, as we have added computers, electronics, transistors, diodes, silicone chip wafers, complex facsimile and data transmission systems, and the many other developments now available for application in the Graphic Arts. This field literally exploded in the post-World War II period. While we do not undertake basic research, we must have scientists and engineers with the creative imagination to develop and apply basic concepts in order to utilize properly the rapid technological changes occurring in the last half of the twentieth century.

We have also developed feedback to the suppliers of our materials and technology to apprise them of our needs and to measure their success in fulfilling those needs. Out of this has grown a testing capability which helps tell us in advance if a material will run efficiently and with required quality, and if not, gives some meaningful clues to our suppliers as to why not.

Safety, as indicated earlier, has always been a real concern of our Company, a responsibility shared by everyone, but spearheaded by a Safety Committee in every manufacturing department, and our record is outstanding. To insure even better performance for millions of hours worked without a lost time accident, safety engineers and industrial hygienists are constantly studying our buildings, equipment, and operations to uncover any possible further improvement. Inspections by the Occupational Safety and Health Administration (OSHA) have shown once more that we are leaders in our industry.

Our engineers have been concerned with pollution since the advent of heatset inks in the 1930s, a great breakthrough which with the contemporary advent of machine coated paper gave magazine and catalog printing such a great technical leap forward. Now we have specialized engineers very knowledgeable in the control and treatment of both water and air effluents.

While the organization to deal with advancing technologies was evolving, so was the overall organization of our Company. Chicago had a unit organization, and, for years, Crawfordsville operated almost as a part of Chicago. There was a resident manager, but his responsibility was greater than his authority. With the advent of more manufacturing divisions, it became evident that each division, including Chicago, must have more authority delegated, supported by its own staffs. All report to Corporate Headquarters in Chicago. There are corporate staffs in Chicago with overall functional and auditing responsibilities. When such a staff cannot be justified at the division level, the corporate staff supplies services to the division.

For many years, it was firmly believed that only a crowded plant could make money, and a diversity of products and services would tend to minimize the ups and downs which could vary between segments of the printing industry. Higher speeds of equipment with attendant greater amounts of materials to be handled changed the first concept, and also the advantages of specialization became more and more evident. Most divisions established since Crawfordsville have concentrated on one type of work, and now Crawfordsville itself is primarily a book plant. This results in a better understanding and knowledge of the customer and his needs. This limitation of size and span of attention has had a most salutary effect on productivity, quality and employee relations. Above all it enables people to know each other and relate as individuals.

A natural outcome of this was the grouping of divisions of like products together under a Group Vice President, who reports to the Executive Vice President. Up to this time, sales were centralized for control purposes in Chicago, though sales offices were located in various parts of the country. Now each Group has its own sales force, although such forces can also sell for other groups, as well as two or more manufacturing divisions or facilities. There is one group each for books, catalogs, directories, and magazines, as well as a Financial Sales unit with manufacturing activities in two groups. The Group Vice Presidents now report to the Executive Vice President for coordination, whereas they formerly reported directly to the Company's President.

FINANCIAL RESOURCES AND CONTROL

Paralleling the Company's growth and development physically, technically, and organizationally was a fourth consideration—maintaining financial strength.

As our business has become more capital intensive, the policy of retaining the large majority of our net earnings in the business has become ever more valuable. Good service based on quality and high productivity, if properly priced, helps our customers prosper and helps us attract new ones, resulting in profits and growth.

Profits and growth are closely interrelated and have been twin objectives for generations. In a closely held company, policies are easily established, executed, and justified.

Following World War II there was a tremendous pent up demand for our services from our customers, as well as opportunities to serve new ones. We expanded as rapidly as we could, in personnel and facilities. Naturally it caused some financial strain. Fortunately, our Treasurer, Gen. C. C. Haffner, Jr., returned to take a most active part in our management, ultimately becoming Chairman. His banking background and expertise in fiscal matters were invaluable in establishing better financial controls, and his business and military experience were equally important in developing our organization to meet new needs and challenges. With the many and varied purchases of this postwar period, he soon turned his attention to developing an adequate appropriation control system, which with some adaptations is still in use. Thus it was possible to know the extent of our commitments, timing of capital needs, and progress of projects.

In 1956, however, it seemed prudent to provide a base for future growth, beyond that possible from retained earnings alone, by a public stock offering of a modest size. Going public put us in a better position for debt financing when and if that was needed. Our continuing policy of retained earnings was clearly indicated, recognized by shareholders then and ever since. Debt financing has been used only sparingly, since profits over the years have maintained a good level for our industry. The shift from a privately held company to a public one was accomplished with little difficulty. At the time I write, the Donnelley family's shareholdings, though diminished in twenty years, continue substantial.

A strong balance sheet continues to be one of our main objectives. Without one, growth could become precarious. Many financial ratios are watched carefully, such as return on sales and investment, and ratios of current assets to current liabilities, working capital to sales, sales to fixed assets, dollars of sales to dollars of wages, and fixed assets to equity.

Budgets, at first admittedly crude, have been used for a long time. An educated guess of sales volume and of manufacturing costs was not a very useful tool for management. Now we have comprehensive marketing studies and long range studies. Each active and potential account is carefully evaluated individually, and combined with others into a sales forecast, usually an ambitious goal. With a tempering of conservatism, this forecast is then used as a basis for manufacturing plans and budgets. All these items are, in turn, reviewed at least semi-annually, more often if changing market conditions indicate. Monthly financial reports comparing actual results with original budget, with budgeted costs at actual volume, and with the prior year's experience by cost center, department, division, group, and the Company as a whole, provide a most useful tool.

In a capital intensive business, a capital budget is particularly necessary, and is likewise prepared annually and reviewed every six months or more often. Based on the detailed studies, forecasts, and contracts, needs for replacement or added equipment and facilities are combined with varying priorities into a total budget related to funds available. The budget also predicts the spending over the years ahead to forecast cash requirements by quarters. It is approved by the Board of Directors, which gives careful consideration to present financial resources and future depreciation and retained earnings. However, each project is subjected to a thorough economic analysis to predict its return on investment. These analyses not only help us to evaluate the desirability of the project, but also establish standards against which we can make later measurements. If the analysis indicates the returns to be insufficient, the project may be revised to remedy this deficiency, or even dropped. Approvals are authorized for different levels of management, with the largest projects submitted to the Board of Directors. Then comes into play the appropriation control procedure mentioned earlier, constantly monitoring that expenditures are according to plan, and finally a comparison of actual and projected results.

We are not endowed with the clairvoyance or other ability to forecast accurately the long term trends of our economy, or the shorter term swings either as to timing or severity. A review of our own history indicates that about twice a decade there is either a slowing or a slight dip in our steady growth in sales and profits. We would be most fortunate if we could time our expansion projects so as to come on stream with an upturn of the economy. However, with often a five-year, or even longer, span of conception, planning, negotiation, design, purchasing, construction, break in, start up, and attainment of a reasonable level of productivity, this is patently most difficult. Our strategy is based on long term confidence in our country's economy and the ability of our customers and ourselves to meet the ever changing needs and challenges of our economy.

Years ago, we recognized that we could not sustain our continued growth pattern by adding a sufficient number of large accounts. The larger portion of printing markets is made up of medium-size and smaller jobs. To penetrate these markets further, we expanded our sales organizations manyfold, developed and located facilities to supply them more efficiently, and modified procedures to handle this type of business more effectively. Competition is more intense in this area, where often we do not have a unique service to offer.

Great are the challenges to increase productivity in every way, maintain and increase quality and adherence to schedule, and sell at a price that represents true value as well as a profit and return on investment. The temptation and pressure are to cut prices and so maintain activity during periods of slack demand, but following this practice has been the ruination of many printers over the years. That we have succeeded is evidenced by the fact that our sales have increased in each of the years following the demise of *Look* and of *Life*, as well as during the last recession, the most severe in decades.

* * *

If we strive to identify and grasp opportunities in the current and future markets, and try to anticipate at least some of the changes to come, at the same time keeping our financial house in order and our organization appropriate to our needs, we should also continue to show the steady, profitable growth essential to the long-range health of the Company.

Conclusion

As we enter the last quarter of the twentieth century, R. R. Donnelley & Sons Company, The Lakeside Press, finds itself in an unquestioned position of leadership in its industry, in size, in financial strength and results, in service in many categories, and by reputation throughout the world. A temptation to rest on one's laurels might be strong, but would be disastrous. The pace of change and technical innovation is increasing, presenting challenges as never before, calling for our utmost in resources and efforts. We are and will continue to be faced with problems of the environment, energy, industrial hygiene, safety, and others. Our attitude should reflect a real sense of humility coupled with courage and justifiable pride. Fortunately, we have the resources, human, financial, and material, to be forward-looking and forward-acting. Above all, there is the unique personality of our Company and the spirit of its people to carry us on well into the future. My firm belief is that our future is best assured if we keep firmly in mind and heart the principles, policies and standards that have guided us so well for over 110 years.

In closing, I cannot do better than quote from my grandmother's perceptive and eloquent remarks at the Company's Sixtieth Anniversary Dinner on October 22, 1924:

"It is not amiss sometimes, I think, to look back on the beginning of an organization, to the early days and to the day of small things. Many times—for as you know, as we grow older we grow very reminiscent—my thoughts turn back to those old days. They were days of struggle, days of self-denial, days of hardship, but they were days of building. When we look at a structure, we see the super-structure in all its proportions and beauty, but how rarely we think of that which lies below the surface or what it cost in thought, effort or patience to lay the foundation so deep, strong, and enduring that the splendid building erected thereon should be a thing of beauty."

She then reminisced of the very early days and the people who started the Company on its tortuous way. She concluded:

"Time will bring many changes. It may be that in the years to come my children and my grandchildren and even my great grandchildren will not be connected with the business that was built on this foundation, and it may perchance be known by another name. My prayer and my desire is that whoever or whatever it may be, wherever it may be, that the spirit of the past will still prevail, and that the spirit of the Golden Rule will still be there and that the institution now and forever will be a synonym for fair dealing, for justice and for honesty."

Our Company obviously is not detached and immune from this increasing rate of change. People and their attitudes and expectations will continue to change. However, biologists tell us that, while the human being can adapt fairly well, he can change only gradually over many generations. This gives me faith that the fundamental values, espoused by people of ability, quality, and integrity, and adapted to our changing society and its needs, will, as in the past, insure the future success of R. R. Donnelley & Sons Company and the thousands who are a part of it.

Printed and bound at
The Lakeside Press,
R. R. Donnelley & Sons Company
Chicago, Illinois and Crawfordsville, Indiana.
Designed by Michael Stancik, Jr.

The type for the text is twelve point Barbou,
which R. R. Donnelley & Sons Company commissioned
the Monotype Corporation Ltd. of London to cut
under the direction of Stanley Morison and John
Dreyfus specially for *The Papers of Benjamin Franklin,*
published by the Yale University Press.
It is based on the *St. Augustin Ordinaire* of Pierre
Simon Fournier, whose types Franklin used in
his press at Passy. In this volume it is combined
with Frederick Goudy's Deepdene series.
The book was printed by web offset lithography.
The paper, Sebago, was made by the S. D. Warren
Company, the vellum cloth for the binding by
The Columbia Mills Incorporated, and the linen cloth
by Joanna Western Mills Company.